The New State of the Economy

The New State
of the Economy

Fred C. Allvine
Fred A. Tarpley, Jr.

Georgia Institute of Technology

Winthrop Publishers, Inc.
Cambridge, Massachusetts

Library of Congress Cataloging in Publication Data

Allvine, Fred C
    The new state of the economy.

    1. United States—Economic conditions—1945–
I. Tarpley, Fred A., joint author.   II. Title.
HC106.7.A37   330.9'73'092   76-58541
ISBN 0-87626-612-X
ISBN 0-87626-611-1 pbk.

© *1977 by Winthrop Publishers, Inc.*
    17 Dunster Street, Cambridge, Massachusetts 02138

10   9   8   7   6   5   4   3   2   1

To Nancy and Carolyn . . .
and to
the memory of Luisa Caroline Tarpley

Contents

chapter seven

The Prophets That Failed   132

chapter eight

Rx for Managing the New State of the Economy   151

Foreword

This is an important and challenging book. The authors present us with the startling thesis that the United States has already passed through its Golden Economic Age! They see the chapter closing on the American dream, the dream of continuous and endless improvement in material conditions. They feel that the American dream was sustained by a few major pillars, and these pillars have collapsed.

The period since the end of the Second World War was one of remarkable economic growth. Incomes were rising, savings were rising, aspirations were rising, expectations were rising, and all of these fed each other. Normal cyclical swings occurred, but they were paled by the dominant upward surge in basic economic parameters. New technologies, cheap energy, American know-how and initiative, and insatiable material desires, all propelled the economy in one direction—up.

Then in the late Sixties and early Seventies a succession of major social tornadoes struck and drastically altered the scene. Consumerism and environmentalism erupted and promised to put costly restraints on the freedom of American business to do what it pleased. Another Middle East war broke out in the early Seventies, forcing an unprecedented increase in the price of oil and almost everything else. Deep shortages appeared in many goods categories, a situation not experienced by American citizens since the end of the Second World War. Waking up at 6 A.M. on cold bitter mornings to queue for 15 minutes for gasoline was a new and traumatizing experience for Americans. Shortages pushed up prices, and inflation became the number one economic problem of the nation. The dollar lost over a third of its value in a few years; real incomes were down and falling. The means the government was forced to use to fight inflation produced one of the deepest peacetime recessions ever experienced, with an unemployment figure of over eight million people. And today the economic policies of the nation are delicately balanced to try to keep at bay the two economic terrors of inflation and unemployment.

Recent years have been characterized by turbulence rather than steady growth, and today's economic picture can change overnight as a result of a distant political, economic, or military development. Business leaders have understandably developed a more cautious attitude toward investing in plant and equipment, in high-risk research and development, and in market expansion. And the public has not recovered its former mood of optimism about endless growth and opportunity. The public is cautious in its spending and less prone to believe in a picture of endlessly increasing affluence.

Fred C. Allvine and Fred A. Tarpley, Jr. have brilliantly researched and documented what they believe to be the end of one economic era and the beginning of a new one. Whether they convince you, the reader, is not the central question. The issues will be debated for years and will be resolved by events rather than by a single, though important, book. The importance of this book lies in the stimulation and challenge it presents to the reader to forge a new understanding of yesterday's major economic forces and today's new economic dilemmas.

This book can be read with profit on three levels. First, Allvine and Tarpley present an exciting data-based account of the major forces shaping the stupendous economic growth of America since the end of the Second World War. They document the rich pool of potential technology and innovation following the war; the pent-up demand; the cheap energy; the favorable government policies; the masterful marketing methods; the unspoiled material values of the American consumer; and the crucial contribution of the automobile, airplane, television, new miracle drugs, and several other major innovations. These developments are described not in dead statistical language, but with force and style to extract their maximum meaning. The reader gets caught up in the drama of well-presented economic history.

On the second level, the book offers a provocative interpretation of the major forces behind the tremendous economic growth in America during the period 1945–1970. This growth was sustained primarily by three forces: an abundant supply of cheap energy, a storehouse of unexploited innovations, and a public attitude that supported growth. And, add the authors, these forces have now been altered in the reverse—and possibly an irreversible—direction. The economy is in a Schumpeterian slump. A dearth of innovations, a constant inflation, and a basic change in consumer confidence and values seem to condemn the nation to a scenario of low or no growth.

And on the third level, the authors offer several recommendations on where this economy has to go. Old ways of thinking and doing business are still very much alive and act to hinder and delay the kind of new thinking that the new economy calls for. The authors point to the need for new economic policies to meet the crisis. They call for vigorous efforts to stimulate competition through structural change; to find ways to bring down energy prices; to redirect the nation's focus to the quality of life and not just the gross national output.

The authors are not prophets of doom. While saying that past attitudes and assumptions will not work, they are also saying that new policies are available which would lengthen and deepen the endowment of this country as it moves toward the twenty-first century. Americans will have to pay more attention to resource conservation, social costs, and quality-of-life considerations than they have in the past. Formerly, we were all happy riding our merry Oldsmobile, mowing our suburban lawns, complaining about "ring-around-the-collar," eating our meat-and-sweet rich diets, and ignoring the poor and the disaffiliated at home and abroad. Now we recognize that no suburb is an island, that everyone's fate is connected, and that a distant military or political development has the potential for painfully disrupting our sheltered lives. The tremendous temptation to avoid the fearful, flee from the obvious, and to yearn for normalcy can be dysfunctional. Allvine and Tarpley, while they have exposed the lost American Dream, are pleading for a sounder vision of the future on which to pin our hopes.

Philip Kotler
Northwestern University

Preface

The poor performance of the economy in the 1970s was the primary factor that motivated the writing of this book. During the first half of the 1970s the United States experienced two back-to-back recessions, the latest one being the most severe since the Great Depression. The disappointing record of the 1970s stands in sharp contrast to the stellar performance of the 1960s.

Various reasons have been advanced to explain our recent economic malaise. One school of thought contends that the economy has been victimized by extreme economic mismanagement. Another holds that one-time shocks such as large-scale crop failures and the rapid escalation in oil prices are the culprits. While economic policies could have been more propitious and the shocks undoubtedly had their effects, we feel that the lackluster performance of our economy is due to more fundamental changes. Our investigations lead us to conclude that the long-run conditions supporting economic growth have diminished in strength, and that this is the primary reason for our poor economic record.

Given the new economic realities, the effect and even the appropriateness of old tools of demand management must be questioned. In place of the continued single-minded dedication to fiscal and monetary policies, attention must be focussed on expanding capacity to produce—the supply side of the economy. The first step in developing these new initiatives is proper diagnosis of the nature of our economic problems. Given proper diagnosis, more appropriate policy prescriptions can be developed. Thus, in the first seven chapters of this book major attention is given to the serious problems existing on the supply side of our economy. Chapter eight is devoted to developing policy prescriptions to give us greater opportunity for economic growth.

The study upon which this book is based could not have been undertaken without the financial support of our business friends. Particular thanks go to Mr. James E. Sadler, Autotronic Systems, Inc.; Mrs. Mary Hudson, Hudson Oil Company; Mr. Ronald J. Peterson, Martin Oil Service, Inc.; Mr. Newell Baker, J. D. Street and Company; and Mr. Ted Orden, Thrifty Oil Company. However, the views expressed in this book do not necessarily represent those of the sponsors.

Mr. David M. Husack was project coordinator and made a major contribution to the study and book. Able assistance was also received from Ms. Pratibha Sherali, Mr. Philip York, and Ms. Nancy Frashuer. Many thanks are due Ms. Betty J. Smith for her helpful suggestions and for her typing of the manuscript.

chapter one

The American Dream Come True

A major change has been working in America. Although largely camouflaged, the transformation to a new way of life has become increasingly and disappointingly visible. From a lavish, expanding flow of new cars, beautiful homes, and other trappings, many Americans are now faced with economic retrenchment.

The American Dream of "the good life," once not only the goal but for many the reality, is quickly diminishing. No longer can the average person expect more real income and goods each year and have these expectations met. Yet for twenty-five years following World War II, this was the American experience. During that period, Gross National Product (measured in constant 1958 dollars) grew from $312 to $722.5 billion, or more than doubled; real income per family increased by almost 90 percent (see Figure 1.1).

Not only did Americans enjoy continually rising incomes, but more of the population could partake of this good life. The winner was the growing middle class that for the first time had a significant measure of discretionary income. A good education was the first

1

FIGURE 1.1: Gross National Product and Per Family Income in 1958 Dollars

Source: *Survey of Current Business.*

step on the road to middle class affluence. Armed with a college degree, one could be assured of a well–paying, respected job, a home set in the suburbs, and a car to offer free movement. Leisure and leisure–time activities, once the privileges of the rich, became increasingly available to the expanding middle class of society. Tennis and golf were favored sports. There was money to buy boats and time to use them. As more strove toward this life and were readily admitted, the ranks of the middle class swelled from 20 percent of the total population in the 1950s to roughly 50 percent in 1970. This segment reached down to offer partial membership to some of the working class. Many of the better paid blue–collar workers could also surround themselves with the trappings of the American dream. The middle class not only became major purchasers of the increasing outflow of goods and services but included in its ranks most of the employees producing them. The constant quest for more and better fostered more products, higher income, and more members for the middle class.

Soon the American Dream of always more and better became a common reality. We were immersed in a life style portrayed in endless programs and commercials on television and radio. The standard by which we gauged our economic success grew under this relentless attack. This reality of the "good life" was converted by many into an expectation—a born right—and became so well inculcated that we failed to see where we came from.

The Changing Scene

The strides in the material quality of life from 1946 to 1970 can be observed from a multitude of statistics. While in 1946, 50 percent of the households had a car, over 80 percent were owners in 1970, and 30 percent had a second car. At the beginning of World War II, 45 percent had mechanical refrigeration; by 1970, it was a rarity for anyone to be without one. The same holds true for a variety of other goods. By 1970, 96 percent viewed their own television; 40 percent could see it in color. Chores were made easier in the 60 percent of households that had automatic clothes washers, 28 percent that had home freezers, and 26 percent that owned dishwashers. The comforts of temperature control were enjoyed by the 41 percent of households that owned room air conditioners. The parade of electric dryers, garbage disposals, electric can openers, electric carving knives, boats and trailers, and private airplanes gave further evidence of a higher standard of living (see Figure 1.2).

Our rapid material growth has also wrought changes in society in nonmaterial ways. The better quality of life was reflected in an increase in life expectancy for men from 64 to 69 years and 68 to 75 for women. Affluence has permitted a wider range of choice,

FIGURE 1.2: Growth in Ownership of Durable Goods

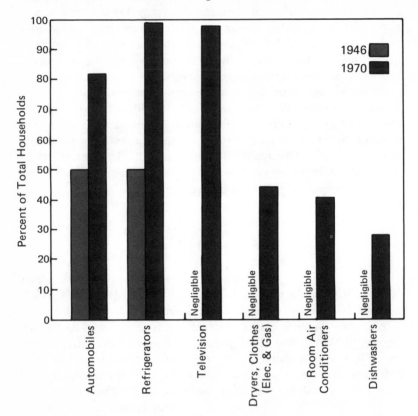

Source: Merchandising Week. Used by permission.

both in occupations and life styles. Job opportunities exploded for engineers, chemists, mathematicians, lawyers, salesmen, doctors, and administrators. Leisure became more abundant and there was a wider variety of ways to entertain oneself. More women engaged in careers, enjoyed a broader social life and greater mobility.

But statistics and bland generalizations mean little, especially to those born during or soon after World War II. And for the older generation, memories of the past are often short and fleeting. An examination of the patterns of social and economic behavior in 1946 and 1970 provide an indication of the magnitude of the change in material well-being.

An important change that took place over the twenty-five-year period after World War II was the increased mobility of the individual and the household, which has resulted in a dramatic alteration of life styles. America became a society on the move until, at the end of this period, approximately one out of every four families moved each year. They did this in pursuit of new job opportunities and from the desire for new ways of living. Leisure activities and shopping alternatives multiplied. A barrel of chicken from the "Colonel," or a hamburger and fries from beneath the Golden Arches, became substitutes for stay-at-home evening meals and Sunday dinner.

Much of this change can be attributed to the automobile. With this creation, one could go anywhere, anyplace, any time. There was no need to fit plans into train schedules, bus departures, or the trolley bell. Instead of waiting in line to buy a ticket, and then enduring an equally long wait for the arrival of the bus or train, you could walk out of the house, get into the car and with a flick of the wrist have an engine at your command. Cities put on new faces as boxy street systems were spanned by criss-crossing urban expressways where, for a time, the flow of traffic was uninterrupted. The suburbs grew. Mothers became part-time chauffeurs, and car pools became as American as apple pie.

In the simpler 1940s families found entertainment in listening to the radio or reading books and magazines. The neighborhood movie house was a once-a-week outing and there were downtown night clubs for dinner, dancing, and big name bands. But both the television and automobile were catalysts for the new leisure pursuits which drew importance away from the city as the center of entertainment. At home, the den became the haven for television watching; portable models went to the beach or campsite. Short weekend trips were no longer considered luxuries as improved highways opened access to retreats in the mountains and at the lakes or ocean. With arrival of the passenger jet the middle class could imitate the travel habits of the rich. Package tours transformed many into world travelers.

For most women, before the War, food preparation, washing and ironing, cleaning, and shopping necessitated a home-centered lifestyle. The typical three good meals a day were prepared from basic ingredients; and there were few, if any, time-saving products such as TV dinners, processed, or frozen foods. Fewer people dined out; no more than one out of ten meals was prepared and consumed outside the home in contrast to one in three today. The two days dedicated to washing and ironing were in large part reclaimed when the washer with hand-operated wringer was replaced by the automatic with a multitude of settings. The dryer made line drying obsolete, and ironing all but disappeared with the arrival of synthetic fabrics. Time-consuming chores yielded to high–powered vacuum cleaners, self–cleaning ovens, disposable plates, napkins, and utensils. No longer judged solely on the appearance of her home, the woman today is more often admired for her activities outside.

At the beginning of the period, a shopper's typical marketing took her almost daily to the butcher shop, bakery, produce stand, and the corner grocery store. Improvements in both the shelf life of products and in home refrigeration have sharply reduced the frequency of shopping. We have moved from the neighborhood store, where credit was extended when the face was familiar, to self-service supermarkets, drugstores, and shopping centers. Here the anonymity of large numbers of customers requires that credit worthiness be attested to by a collection of plastic cards furnished by banks, retailers, and oil companies. Instead of the trips by streetcar or bus to "go downtown" for clothing and major purchases, the suburbanite now relies on his automobile for jaunts to outlying shopping centers, discount stores, and drive-in convenience stores. In this aspect of life, the central city has also declined in importance.

The New Reality

From these contrasts in basic areas of American living, the vast transformation of society is apparent. Although the change has been extremely rapid relative to early eras, the many who share the easy life of automatic appliances and automobiles have barely perceived the pace or extent. Most persons, bombarded daily by change, have developed an immunity and find progress gradual. Yet, change is American, and the change in America was wrought by a proliferation of new creations such as the automobile, a wealth of natural and human resources, and a change in social attitudes which both accommodated to and caused more change.

It is unfortunate, though, that recent events have reversed the direction of change and brought frustration and hardship rather than more wealth and ease of living. Although this reversal has not been as sudden as it seems, it is pervasive. Hitting hard at all segments of the population, this new economic trend has put a particularly hard squeeze on the middle class.

But now the ride is over, and all segments of the population have been hit hard. From 1973 to 1974 the purchasing power of the middle class dollar dropped 6 percent as the cost of transportation, housing, and food rose sharply; personal taxes rose 26.5 percent. Since the middle-class accounts for approximately 75 percent of consumer purchases, which are especially heavy in the durable goods sector, the loss of disposable middle-class income is a serious threat to the economy. Many families cut discretionary spending and took second jobs to keep pace with basic living expenses. Beset by cutbacks, layoffs, inflation, higher taxes, and a general decline in a standard of living they had come to take for granted, many in the middle class find the loss of the "good life" shattering.

Equally devastating has been the recent experience of the youth of today, particularly college graduates who are aspiring to enter the affluent middle class ranks. Many knock but few are admitted as entry is no longer automatic. Even those admitted find that they are less well off than they had anticipated. This comes as quite a shock to those who have prepared their way carefully with four years spent in college. Further reinforcing the expectation of the good life were the visible abundances the youth saw or experienced during their formative years. Political speeches and talks by economists told the American people repeatedly that theirs was the richest nation in the world. Of course, the existence of occasional recessions was recognized, but the forecast of these authorities was normally onward and upward after only a brief period of adjustment.

After playing the game by the rules, the youth were faced with the first evidence of change when they tried to obtain a good white collar job. While a few years earlier employers were fighting for applicants' attention, recently students have found that their newly acquired skills are received with almost an air of indifference. They are startled by prospective employer's questions of what can you do for the company and why do you deserve a job offer. Gone are the days when college graduates were courted with multiple plant trips, dined in expensive restaurants, and given several job offers. The change from a seller's to a buyer's market for qualified college grads is symbolic of fundamental changes occurring in the economy. Exemplifying this trend, a recent study has revealed that 9.3 percent of 1972 graduates lacked work in October 1972 while only 1 percent of 1958 graduates lacked work in October 1958. This compared poorly with the national unemployment figure of 5.6 percent overall. Even for high school graduates unemployment was lower at 7.7 percent. Obviously, a college education is not the ticket it used to be.

For those fortunate enough to obtain a white collar job, it means much less than it did ten years ago. White–collar workers are subject to layoffs and firings once reserved for blue–collar workers, and the financial rewards associated with entry level jobs are no longer there. While once a college education was a good long-term investment, now the expenditure, in terms of future income, needs to be carefully evaluated. The gap in earnings potential between a person going on to four years of college and his friend who takes a blue–collar job after high school is small. At today's inflated prices, a new white collar worker can no longer make a down payment on a new home and new car, nor will he be showered with oil company and bank credit cards once mailed out indiscriminately. Many college graduates continue to live in the often impoverished circumstances they experienced during college years.

It is hard for many—the young and their elders as well—to release their hold on the American dream, but release it they must. The forces that created and supported it are gone.

chapter two

The Twenty-Five-Year Rocket Ride

At the end of World War II, there was fear that the United States would return to the dark days of the Great Depression of the 1930s. This was not to be; instead a new economic dawn unfolded for the nation. Conditions coalesced, creating for the economy a twenty-five-year period of unparalleled material transformation. Buoyed by an *abundant supply of cheap energy,* a *storehouse of unexploited innovations,* and a *public attitude that supported growth,* this transformation to the "good life" began.

None of the three basic sources of the twenty-five-year rocket ride would have been sufficient on its own to propel the growth of material affluence to the extent that occurred. It was the happy convergence and mutual support of these three forces that made it all possible. Cheap and abundant supplies of energy had existed before World War II, but their full utilization had not been realized. However, the new production processes developed during and after the war were largely energy intensive. As machines replaced men, the energy requirement per unit of output increased. Trends in consumption aided and abetted the process. The abundance and cheapness of energy when compared with the high cost of labor encouraged the development of energy-intensive, but labor-saving technologies. Energy and technology worked together to increase the outpouring of goods and services which generated our growing standard of living.

The union of social values with technological innovations and energy resources is more subtle but no less important. Social values determine what will be encouraged and what will be proscribed. Not only did social attitudes support the use of energy and technological efforts, but a progrowth ethic, such as we enjoyed, worked to direct and encourage further activities. In the United States the quarter century following the war saw considerable emphasis placed on innovation. In the public's mind, what was new was better; a product that could do more or take less time was highly lauded. The consumption of energy both for the production of these products and for their use was also gladly sanctioned.

The favorable public attitude in combination with energy and technology have been the triad of forces fueling the meteoric rise of the U.S. economy; their interactive nature cannot be overemphasized. Though this book will proceed to tackle individually the development of each fundamental force, it must be remembered that it was their convergence which fed our increasing affluence.

War-related research and production had bequeathed America with a storehouse of technology. Many of the techniques and products developed during the conflict were easily transferable to a peacetime economy. One of the greatest legacies of the war period was the development of research focused toward the accomplishment of a particular goal. Industry believed that technological advance could be secured by proper application of men and capital. Innovations developed during, or after, the war, using the techniques of controlled research and development, improved the efficiency of production, distribution, and marketing of goods and services. The American worker was able to produce more products of better quality in a shorter period of time. During the last twenty-five years, a threefold increase of output per man-hour in the manufacturing sector and a fourfold increase on the farm have been experienced. At the levels of the household and individual wage earner, the progress in productivity translated into greater real income.

The second way in which technology contributed to the expanding economy was through the development of new and improved products and services. From electric blenders to massive computers, new products filled gaps in everyday life. Life was better because we had these new products. The warm reception that these goods received from the American public further stimulated output.

Aside from the direct technological advances achieved, the overall knowledge and ability of the labor force had been expanded. In the initial stages of the war, thousands of people were trained in skills that were in short supply. These skills proved to be just as valuable to industrial production during peacetime.

Most of the industries employing new technologies were large energy consumers. As inanimate energy developed from coal, natural gas, petroleum, and electricity was increasingly substituted for animal and human effort, the amount of energy employed per worker approximately doubled from 1946 to 1970. Large inputs of energy were also required to operate many of the new products: Air conditioning had become standard for the middle class home and for businesses. The privately owned automobile was a major energy consumer. Jetting off to a vacation in the sun, escaping to the mountains for skiing, and traveling on short weekend jaunts were made possible by increasing expenditures of energy.

The extent to which energy nourished the United States' growing standard of living is reflected in our consumption of 35 percent of the world's fuel, although we are only 6 percent of the world's people. Total energy consumption increased 104 percent from 1946 to 1970 while the United States' population increased only 42 percent and the United States' real Gross National Product (GNP) increased 131 percent.

This vast use of energy was encouraged by its seemingly boundless supply and cheap prices. At the end of World War II, the United States was certainly energy rich. This country was not only the world's largest producer of oil and, as such, self-sufficient, it was also a net exporter. Natural gas was so plentiful that much of it was flared off as a waste by-product in the process of producing oil, and there was such an abuandance of coal that estimates of reserves ran as high as 1,000 years at then current rates of use. During this period, the United States consumed increasing quantities of energy at prices that were often constant or falling. With such energy resources, the fueling of the economy was indeed assured.

Underlying the technological advances and extensive use of cheap, plentiful energy was a public attitude amenable to growth. Although most economists in the immediate post World War II period forecasted a return to the economic despair of the 1930s, the American public, deprived by wartime shortages, was eager to spend. The government took early action to guard against a return to the prewar depression. With the Employment Act of 1946, responsibility was vested in the Government to foster a high level of employment and oversee the allocation of resources. A council of economic advisors was established to advise the President on economic policy, and the Joint Economic Committee was given legislative mandate to carry out the spirit of the Act. These actions codified the belief that man could control his economic destiny.

At the end of the War, the Federal government lent its support to other programs stimulating the economy. Federally–insured VA and FHA loans made it possible for savings and loan institutions to finance a rapid expansion of home construction at low interest rates, bringing home ownership to a broad cross section of the population. Federal policy also supported credit expansion for the purchase of other consumer durable goods, such as automobiles and appliances.

The typical American was more than willing to accept the goods and services produced by a growing economy and to discount the problems. Few questioned the social and environmental costs. The degradation of our water and air resources, inadequate health and safety of industrial workers were mainly fears to be addressed in the future. We rarely doubted the propriety of tearing down homes and balkanizing communities to construct expressways. Smokestacks and congested roadways were seen as the results of success, not admissions of failure. The quest for more—the race to produce and consume—was a way of life.

These three interrelated factors wove such a strong base for American prosperity that the economy did not experience any serious slump from 1946 to 1970. There were, however, five mild eco-

FIGURE 2.1: Length of Post World War II Recessions

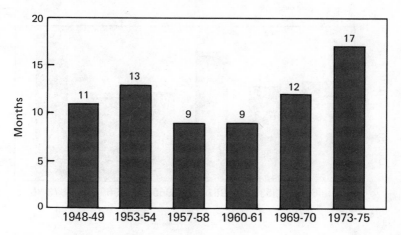

Source: Survey of Current Business.

nomic downturns, labeled the recessions of 1948–1949, 1953–1954, 1957–1958, 1960–1961, and 1969–1970. These were short-term declines and only temporarily retarded the growth of American prosperity (see Figure 2.1).

The 1973–1975 Recession

All of the basic indicators of economic activity show that America entered a downturn in late 1973 that was more severe than any of the five earlier postwar recessions. The length of the slump has been longer, and the decline of industry output and GNP has been steeper (see figures 2.1, 2.2, and 2.3). The rate of unemployment was higher than at any time since World War II (see Figure 2.4).

The stockmarket, the common financial barometer of the economy, has dropped precipitously. Value Line, a composite of more than 1,500 stocks, fell from an early 1969 high of $180 per share to $30 per share in late 1974—a decline of 72 percent (see Figure 2.5).

FIGURE 2.2: Decline in Industrial Output During Post World War II Recessions

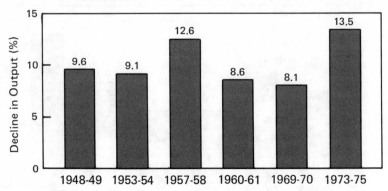

Source: *Survey of Current Business.*

The Dow Jones Industrial Average of 30 major stocks declined from $1,052 in early 1973 to $577 in December 1974. This was the most rapid erosion of investor wealth since the crash of 1929. Along with the economy, consumer confidence collapsed to the lowest point since World War II (see Figure 2.6 on p. 17).

The seriousness of our economic situation in recent years is highlighted by other statistics as well. Housing starts fell to the lowest level since the end of World War II in 1975, and the production of automobiles declined to the lowest level in more than a decade. In the industrial sector, trucking experienced its sharpest relative decline since the war. The Federal government recorded its largest peacetime budget deficit in fiscal years 1975 and 1976 (see Figure 2.7 on p. 18). The year 1974 will be remembered as the year when the United States experienced double digit inflation and near double digit unemployment. With real income at pre-1970 levels, there were fewer discretionary dollars to spend on durable goods which are so important to the momentum of the economy. The American people wondered what went wrong and whether the economy would recover.

Quite naturally, questions were addressed to the prophets of prosperity—the economics profession. The twenty-five years of con-

FIGURE 2.3: Decline in Gross National Product During Post World War II Recessions

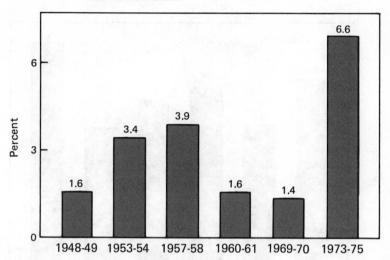

Source: Survey of Current Business.

tinual prosperity following the war were good to the profession as well as the public in general. Its stature and prestige advanced with the progress of the economy. Economic policy makers in Washington became confident they could act when needed to keep the economy growing. Their primary tools were fiscal policy—spending or taxation—and monetary policy—expanding or contracting the money supply. The mildness of the five short post-World War II economic downturns led the economists to speak of "fine tuning" the economy. Unfortunately, they were not deserving of public trust and their own self-confidence. It was the robustness of the economy that carried the day, not the economists with their abstract theories, models, and prescriptive policies. Rather than developing relevant models to form a basis for concrete policies, they have squandered their time on unrealistic abstractions. Now with the country beset by so many problems, economists have few insights to offer. In disarray, they lack agreement about what has gone wrong and how to stage a sustained recovery. In the quibbling about the origin of our difficulties, blame is quickly transferred to policy makers.

FIGURE 2.4: Highest Level of Unemployment During Post World War II Recessions

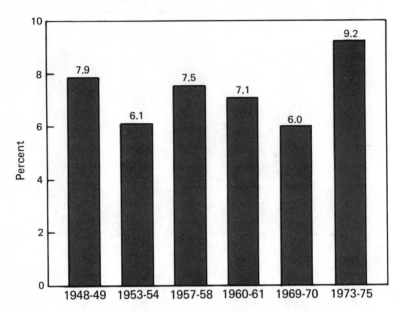

Source: *Survey of Current Business.*

This book presents a different argument. No longer are the three conditions that propelled our economy in the postwar boom favorable to rapid growth. Technology, energy sources, and social attitudes, no longer lend the strong support they once did. Many of the easier technologies have been discovered and exploited. New economic innovations are needed to bolster the economy, but these are harder to find and will require more intensive and costly research and development effort. Although some forms of energy are still in large supply, their location and cost of development are expensive obstacles to their use. Social attitudes have also taken an about-face: The progrowth ethic has been transformed into one concerned with the costs of America's industrialization and household waste.

Most people presume that the recent recession of 1973–1975 was

FIGURE 2.5: The Value Line Composite Average (More than 1500 stocks)

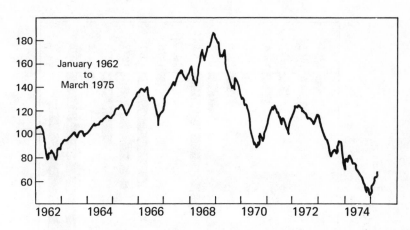

Source: Value Line Investment Service. Used by permission.

FIGURE 2.6: Index of Consumer Confidence

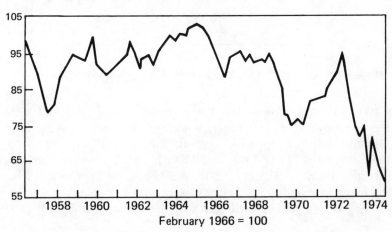

February 1966 = 100

Source: Survey Research Center, University of Michigan. Used by permission.

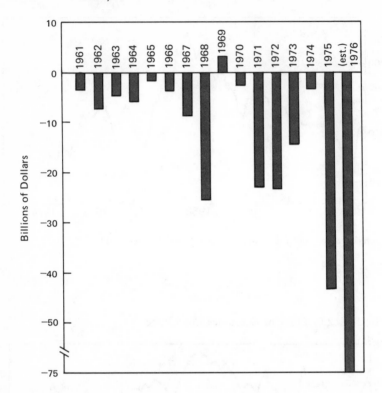

Source: U.S. Department of Commerce, Bureau of Economic Analysis.

a temporary condition and that opportunities would rebound with the economy. There is danger, however, that such thinking is a Candide-like game in self-deception. America will not return to the boom years of the 1950s and 1960s but experience, instead, an extended period of slower growth. But before the economy can be stabilized, economists and policy makers must recognize the sources of our past economic growth and why these sources no longer provide support. They must turn from studying the short-run, symptomatic problems to analyzing fundamental causes. Once this is done, a sound basis can be established for leading the economy forward.

In the following chapters, the supports to the twenty-five-year economic boom will be studied and analyzed in more detail.

chapter three

From a Progrowth
to a Conservation Ethic

Of the three major forces that were responsible for the twenty-five-year rocket ride—a storehouse of unexploited innovations, cheap and abundant energy resources, and a progrowth societal ethic—the latter is surely the least tangible. This, however, does not detract from its importance. The period from the end of World War II to 1970 saw a transforming of social values from a set that not merely accommodated but actually promoted economic growth to one that generated resistance to the growth process.

At the beginning of this period, the United States was feeling its collective oats. After ten years of depression and five years of war, the American public was looking forward to consuming the material goods that they had so long been denied. Continued self-denial held very little fascination, and the prospect of material abundance was viewed with uncritical acclaim. The smoke coming out of the chimneys of industrial America became a symbol of the production of goods and services and the availability of jobs. The resources of nature, the labor force, and the marketplace were viewed as the ingredients for producing a more abundant tomorrow, given the mood of the day. Economic growth was seen as an unassayed good.

By the end of this twenty-five-year period, societal values were in the midst of dramatic change. Society had recognized production as a two-edged sword; in producing material goods, we also produce negative side effects. The same smokestacks that earlier signified our material progress were viewed as belching behemoths that obscured the sun and threatened both body and soul. The earth's natural resources were no longer viewed as a frontier to be subjugated by man; conservation was no longer a luxury but a necessity.

A primary reason for change in societal values was the economic success of the twenty-five-year rocket ride. Concern over the environment, human resources, and marketing practices is a luxury that tends to increase as affluence rises. The poor and indolent are not concerned with such esoteric problems. The environmental crusades of the 1960s were most often led by the children of affluence. Additionally, because we were producing more goods at the end of this period, we were also producing more adverse side effects. In 1970, our stock of automobiles was almost four times what it had been at the beginning of the period. The resulting problems of congestion, emissions, and safety demanded increasing public attention. The very act of packaging our increasing material abundance made problems of its own. The convenience of the disposable can or bottle, the plethora of throwaway paper goods, and all sorts of fancy packaging leads to the ever more costly problems of dealing with the growing mountains of solid waste, both in money and environmental terms. Finally, there has also been increasing recognition that prosperity was purchased by large infusions of depletable natural resources. This was especially the case with energy resources. Our petroleum and natural gas resources have been severely dented in support of the twenty-five-year rocket ride.

The farm boy of the late 1940s was looking toward the city both as a land of greater opportunity and as an escape from what he saw as the confines of rural life. In contrast, in the late 1960s the pampered progeny of suburban affluence was preaching a doctrine of return to nature. The factory job that had been seen as an escape from the bleakness and hardships of farm work in the 1940s was, by the end of the period, being attacked under the rubric of the blue collar malaise.

By the middle 1960s, we had begun to question the very basis of the American society in several areas at the same time. Activists such as Ralph Nader, Martin Luther King, the Sierra Club, and Common Cause led protests to expose and expound upon those aspects of current American culture which they found to be wrong. There can be little question that much of their message was needed and useful. The net effect of their combined efforts, as communicated to us incessantly by the broadcast and press media, was to cause us collectively to question what had been fundamental commitments. In the areas of air and water pollution, human rights, safety, and the rights of consumers, laws were passed in great profusion. Figure 3.1 shows that, beginning in the middle 1960s, we attempted, at an ever-accelerating pace, to correct problems—real

FIGURE 3.1: Federal Consumer Protection Laws, 1890–1972

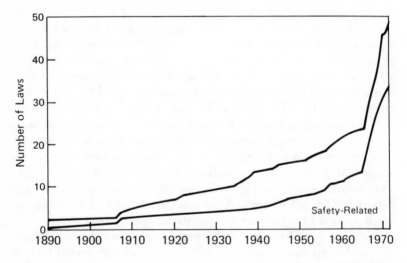

Source: National Business Council for Consumer Affairs, "Safety in the Marketplace," *Action Guidelines,* September 1972, p. 210. Used by permission.

and imagined—in the environment, in the area of human resources, and in marketing practices.

Just as material progress is a two-edged sword by which the production of goods also produces undesirable side-effects, laws have a similar duality: the same law that attempts to control pollution may also control production; the law that attempts to make sure that dangerous drugs are not introduced into the market may deter and delay the introduction of life-extending drugs; and the same law that tries to insure that a person is not denied employment because of race, age, religion, or sex may adversely affect and perversely complicate the employment process. Individually these laws were aimed at specific problems; collectively they may retard economic growth.

We shall examine the effects of these changing societal values in terms of the environment, human resources, and marketing practices. Society is increasingly utilizing its resources to insure that the productive process is safe, clean, and just. More is no longer equated with better; production is not an end in and of itself, but one among many competing societal values.

Pollution

The process by which changing societal values influence society's attitudes toward economic growth is best illustrated in the problem of pollution. For most of our existence, the natural environment has been considered as a free good to be used and in many cases abused for man's benefit. Air and water were the least expensive sewers available. The United States was born under conditions where land and natural resources were cheap, and capital and labor were expensive. One of the heritages of this past has been a view that nature's bounty was there for man to plunder.

Much of the environmental abuse observed in the United States is related to an almost insatiable desire for energy. From the past, when much of our virgin forests were denuded to provide charcoal for our embryonic steel production, to the present, when much of West Virginia and eastern Kentucky are either slag heap or bear the scars of surface mining, the extraction, conversion, and consumption of energy resources have contributed to environmental degradation. The twenty-five-year rocket ride was fueled by enormous amounts of energy. Emerging technologies tended to be energy-intensive and contributed to doubling our energy usage between 1946 and 1970. Unfortunately, in doubling the production of energy we more than doubled the environmental costs that were associated with the extraction, conversion, and consumption of energy. As energy uses grew, so did the wastepile, so did the slag heap, and so did the air and water pollution associated with each stage of this process.

In economic terms pollution is a negative externality—negative because it is harmful, external because the costs do not fall on the polluter. As our economy grew, pollution grew abreast. Increasingly, the real, and often intangible, costs of this pollution were imposed upon members of society. Air quality in our major cities deteriorated, and we were faced with warnings that breathing this air could be dangerous to our health, especially if we were either very young or very old. Several beaches near major cities became so polluted from municipal sewage and industrial waste that they had to be closed. Fishing diminished in a number of rivers, lakes and coastal waters since either the fish were contaminated or the water had insufficient oxygen to support aquatic life. Oil spills from meeting our energy demands also destroyed resort areas.

In the 1960s, the extent and danger of pollution became increasingly obvious. The frequent smog alerts in Los Angeles, when children were kept off school playgrounds; the Santa Barbara oil spill, where beautiful beaches were ruined, and birds and other wildlife died by the hundreds of thousands; and the Japanese epidemic of mercury poisoning were poignant symbols of man's gross misuse of the earth. As people were sensitized to the effects of pollution on their daily lives, they became less and less willing to bear the costs that polluters had gratuitously shifted to them. What began as a few voices crying in, and for, the wilderness soon became a loud chorus demanding that those who caused the pollution should stop the pollution. In economic terms, this was an attempt to internalize the costs of pollution—to force the polluters to pay for pollution-abatement equipment rather than have society pay in terms of environmental degradation.

In a frontier economy, there are few environmental problems. Waste can readily be absorbed by existing streams, and smoke from the cooking fire can be dispersed over the abundant landscape. The capacity that natural systems have to regenerate themselves can be depended upon to solve the problems of pollution. But as we move from a frontier type of economy toward our present-day economy, we see that this natural regenerative capacity is reached and breached with regard to many types of pollution. Recently, the term "ecology" has been introduced into the everyday vernacular. The ecologists stress the interrelatedness of natural systems. Their fervent message is that we are in danger of overloading these systems to such an extent that they will no longer operate in the way on which we have come to depend. They see the earth as a closed system. Our air, water, and land resources both individually and collectively are in grave danger.

Among major sources of air pollution, the automobile takes first place. The internal combustion engine used in the United States today is less than 25 percent efficient in utilizing the energy in the fuel it burns. This means that in addition to providing our basic form of transportation, it also produces copious quantities of certain undesirable by-products such as carbon monoxide, hydrocarbons, and nitrogen oxide. Unfortunately, both individually and in combination with natural and synthetic gases, these by-products impose a serious danger to man and man's property. Automobile emissions, especially when they are combined with the emissions of other sources of pollution such as industrial plants, utilities, and trash incinerators, become smog. Smog obscures the landscape and inflames both eyes and lungs of many city dwellers.

In addition to the problems with air pollution, equally serious problems exist with our water resources. As our economy industrialized and we were transformed from a rural to an urban and suburban society, the natural capacity of our water resources to dispose of the increased waste was quickly overtaken. Our Great Lakes are vast sinkholes for undiluted wastes such as metal salts, sewage, and the garbage of man and machine. Despite large expenditures on water treatment and sewage facilities, the increasing wastes—human, industrial, and agricultural—have become almost unmanageable.

The exploitation of timber, coal, and petroleum resources is the principal cause of land deterioration. Early in our history, large areas of forest were cleared without any attention being given to replanting. Much of the natural topsoil eroded, reducing the fertility of the land and silting our streams and rivers. In attempting to feed our increasingly voracious appetite for energy, further indignities were practiced upon the landscape. Strip mining is extremely efficient in that, after stripping the overburden off the coal, direct access with very large machinery minimizes the labor and capital costs per ton. Unfortunately, an area that has been strip mined often resembles the landscape of the moon. Until recently, very little attention was given to reclaiming the land after the coal resources had been stripped. The ocean areas of the continental shelf of the United States have been breached to supply our ever-increasing need for petroleum and natural gas resources. Careless drilling and shipping and the resultant blowouts, leaks, and spills have had various disastrous effects, not only on our coastal recreational areas but also on their ecology.

Legislation for Pollution Control

Although the problems associated with pollution were recognized in the late 1940s, attempts to confront the problems were left primarily to the states. Federal agencies, to the extent that they were involved, dealt mostly with investigation and research, not regulation. It was not until 1956 that the first federal incursion was made into the problems of water pollution control. The Water Pollution Control Amendment of 1956 was significant primarily because it instituted a federal presence. The states still retained the responsibility for pollution control and the enforcement process proved both ineffectual and cumbersome. In the mid-1960s, additional legislation was passed to deal with the increasingly recognized problems of air and water pollution. The setting of standards was still primarily a state responsibility. A state had the burden of proof to show that an individual polluter did not meet stated air and water standards.

It was only in the late 1960s and, more importantly, in the early 1970s that stronger steps were taken toward pollution abatement and control. States or regions were still allowed to set standards, but these standards had to meet certain federal minimums. The new spirit of cracking down on polluters was contained in the Clean Air Amendments of 1970 and the Water Pollution Act Amendments of 1972.

The Clean Air Amendments of 1970 declared that any and all atmospheric pollution was illegal. The burden of proof had moved from the prosecution to the defense, and special zoning and other partial controls of pollution were no longer permitted. The Environmental Protection Agency (EPA) was given independent status and the power to enforce the new law. This agency was mandated to establish acceptable standards for the various classes of air pollution such as hydrocarbons, carbon monoxide, nitrogen oxide, sulfur dioxides, and photochemical oxidants. The states were required to translate these new federal standards into emission limits for particular industrial plants and utilities. The act established stringent emission levels for automobiles. A reduction of 90 percent in certain pollutants by 1975 was required. The EPA was given considerable discretionary power in imposing standards on any substance which it found to be injurious to health, such as mercury and lead.

The second piece of major legislation, the Water Pollution Act Amendments of 1972, expressly stated that no one has the right to pollute our waterways. This was a drastic departure from earlier legislation that attempted to set limits on how much pollution would be allowed. The main goal of the new legislation was to secure a zero level of discharge by 1985. Interim goals were also set. By 1976, polluters must install the most practical technology available to control pollutants. The 1983 goal requires the installation of the best available technology. As mentioned previously, by 1985 a zero level discharge of pollutants was prescribed. The EPA was armed with the power to levy fines, issue subpoenas, and sue to insure that these guidelines were met. The shifting of the burden of proof from the government to the polluter is seen as a major step in facilitating the EPA's enforcement program.

These laws are the manifestation of public concern over the environment. The mandates of these laws impose tough standards on would-be polluters. The legislation is specific, both as to limits and to deeds. The intent of the laws is to internalize the costs of pollution control by requiring municipalities, automobile owners, industries, and utilities to treat or eliminate the pollutants that they dump into both air and water. The air and water are no longer to be treated as free goods subject to the convenience of the polluter.

There can be little question about the desirability of securing clean air and water. There is, however, a real question about cost. It is estimated, for example, that reducing the water discharge rate to zero would cost twice as much as reducing it to the 5 percent discharge level. By placing the cost on those who create the pollution, a certain equity is surely realized, but there is also little doubt that these costs will in many cases be passed on to consumers through higher prices, utility rates, and taxes.

Press and government documents have been full of numbers estimating the costs of achieving a clean environment. Unfortunately, there is great variation in the figures given and the items included. A 1973 report of the Federal Council on Environmental Quality estimates that the cost of air pollution control, including the cost of requiring automobiles to comply with the standards, will be between $135 and $140 billion for the period from 1972 to 1985, or some $11 billion a year. The National Water Commission estimates the cost to meet the 1983 goal of utilizing the best available technology for water pollution control to be $200 billion for the period from 1972 to 1983. This estimate, however, does not include the cost associated with dealing with water pollution problems caused by mining, farming, and urban runoff. If these additional items are included, then this estimate must be increased to $335 billion, or some $30 billion per year. A Brookings Institution study estimates that the total cost for pollution control between 1972 and 1985 will be $500 billion. This would mean that toward the end of the period an estimated $60 billion a year will be spent for pollution control.

By whatever measure we use, attempts to insure clean air and water are utilizing a large amount of our resources. In percentage terms the figures given are relatively modest, but the impact of these expenditures may be much greater. These laws mandate that industries, utilities, and local government units spend billions of dollars for pollution control. While there are real benefits to a cleaner environment, the fact still remains that the resources employed in this effort are not available to increase our capital stock. In the 1970s the United States lags behind most western nations in the percentage of its gross national product that it is dedicating to capital formation. Capital used for pollution control is capital unavailable for expansion of productive capacity. According to a McGraw-Hill survey, industry spent some 6.2 percent of its total capital expenditure in 1974 on pollution control equipment, and this percentage is expected to increase in future years. In particular industries such as the Kraft paper industry, more than one-fourth of all capital expenditures is for pollution control.

During the twenty-five-year period from 1946 to 1970, a dramatic change in societal values took place as they related to problems of degradation of air, water, and land resources. Now the public attitude is moving from one of little concern for these problems to one where eradicating them is a high national priority. An increasing portion of society's resources is being diverted from increasing our ability to produce more goods to reducing our capacity for producing more bads. This, in many cases, is undoubtedly a desirable reallocation of resources. But it must be realized that, just as pollution imposes costs to society, so too does controlling that pollution. These costs are in terms of higher prices for goods and services, higher tax rates, and a reduced capacity to produce, which in turn may cause even higher prices. Just as environment is not a free good, neither is environmental control.

Human Resources

The reasons for the high level of economic attainment of the American society are many—very important is the infusion of large quantities of raw materials, especially energy resources. Another ingredient of that success is that the American work force has traditionally been productive, and one of the reasons for the high level of output has surely been the American worker's dedication to the work ethic. Additionally, the American industrial worker has been aided by ever increasing inputs of capital. Since

1946, American business has accelerated the substitution of capital outlay for the ever more expensive labor resource. "Automation" helped workers to produce more and also to increase their real income.

During the latter stages of the twenty-five-year rocket ride, fundamental changes in the perception of work and of what the employment process should do occurred in the United States. The job was no longer seen as a simple economic relationship between employer and employee. The employment process came to be viewed as a way for society to solve many of its social problems. Society felt an increasing need to intervene in the employment process. The problems of health and safety at work and of the need for equal access to job opportunities merited societal and governmental concern. But just as in the case of the environmental issue, this increased concern may cause almost as many problems as it attempts to solve. There can be little doubt that both legislation attempting to correct the problems of occupational health and safety, and federal standards regulating recruitment, hiring, and promotion of workers, have increased the complexity and the cost of doing business.

Occupational Safety and Health

Americans have been interested in working conditions since the turn of the century. For example, attempts to end the abuses of child labor, sweatshops, and dangerous and unhealthful work sites have been a part of American labor history for over fifty years. The increased attention that occupational health and safety received in the late 1960s and early 1970s was not only a difference in degree but in kind. The truth of the matter is that the working environment in many industries is extremely dangerous to the safety and health of the worker. This is in part due to the creation of industrial hazards by rapid technological progress; in addition, there is a lack of concern and of adequate standards on the part of business.

The statistics on death and injury occurring in connection with work are disheartening. The National Safety Council estimates that each year some 14,000 workers die and over two million receive injuries that disable them at least temporarily. The cost of these accidents and deaths in terms of lost man hours of work, medical

expenses, workmen's compensation, and insurance is real and large—
in excess of ten billion a year. When we add to these figures the
less tangible but equally real costs associated with occupational illnesses caused by exposure to toxic substances or continued exposure
to high levels of noise and heat, the figure increases greatly. In certain industries, such as underground coal mining, meat packing,
logging, and construction, the injury and sickness rates are several
times the average. Until the late 1960s, there was very little federal
concern with occupational health and safety. Most of the setting and
enforcement of the existing standards was left to the states, and there
were large variations in both the quality of the standards and the
enforcement.

Early in the Johnson administration, federal safety and health
legislation was proposed. It was not until seventy-nine miners were
killed in a 1968 coal mine explosion that national attention was
focused on these issues. The legislative response was the Coal Mine
Health and Safety Act of 1969 and later the much broader Occupational Safety and Health Act of 1970.

The Coal Mine Health and Safety Act imposed rigid and expensive standards on coal mines. These standards were established to
prevent transportation accidents and cave-ins and to reduce the
possibility of explosions and fires caused by gas within the mine.
The incidence of diseases related to the inhalation of coal dust,
such as black lung disease, was also a concern of these regulations.
The effect of this new legislation on coal mine operations has been
a subject of controversy among coal operators, the Department of
Interior, and the United Mine Workers. Many small coal operators
closed their mines because they could neither afford nor finance
the investments necessary to meet the standards set by the act. One
of the effects of the act has been to reverse the trend of increasing
productivity in the coal industry. Productivity which had been increasing at 3 percent a year is now some 20 percent below the 1969
figure. One high-ranking executive in the coal industry estimates
that the act has added $1.50 to the price of a ton of coal. Decreases
in productivity are primarily the result of the larger crews that are
required, the more frequent work stoppages to test for gas and unsafe conditions, and the great amount of shoring and other activities
to reduce the danger of cave-ins.

The Occupational Safety and Health Act (OSHA) requires the Labor Department to set safety and health standards for all workers who had not been covered by previous legislation. These standards apply to nearly five million businesses which employ more than sixty million workers. The Occupational Safety and Health Administration is required to set standards that deal with every aspect of a firm's operation, from plant design, materials handling, protective clothing, medical facilities, and machinery safeguards to the level of toxic substances in the air, such as asbestos dust, and even to the amount of noise and heat associated with the work process. OSHA inspectors are empowered to make spot inspections and to close down any operation that does not meet OSHA standards. These inspectors also conduct investigations into fatalities or injuries or in response to employee complaints.

The bureaucratic task imposed on OSHA was truly monumental. Standards had to be set for equipment, clothing, medical facilities, and so forth, and in many cases on the basis of limited and often contradictory data. The resulting standards are testimony to the tenacity of a budding bureaucracy. Hundred page manuals classifying various kinds of stepladders are but one of the products of a bureaucratic state. The act imposes expensive programs of maintenance and record keeping on employers. It is difficult to secure an exact figure for all the cost involved, and certainly part of the cost will be recovered in reduced rates of employee accidents and sickness. One estimate is that 3.3 percent of total new capital investment in manufacturing industries between 1975 and 1978 will be spent to comply with the new standards.

These estimates are very uncertain, as standards for toxic substances and acceptable noise and heat levels are incomplete. Occupational illnesses result from chronic exposure to these varied job hazards. A much larger number of workers die from occupational illnesses—a hundred thousand annually—than from accidental death on the job. OSHA has recently determined the appropriate level of exposure to such airborne toxic substances as polyvinyl chloride, asbestos, and lead. The cost of OSHA regulations on industries involved in the manufacture of these substances could be extremely high. OSHA is now attempting to set standards for allowable noise and heat, but unfortunately, the available data are minimal. A standard of eighty decibels, for example, may cost two-and-a-half to three times as much to obtain as one of ninety decibels.

The minimization of accidents and health hazards associated with a job is a desired good and no doubt much of the legislation passed in the late 1960s and early 1970s will be paid for at least in part by improved health and safety. But the effect of this legislation is to channel investment funds away from increasing productive capacity toward reducing hazards. When the percentage of new capital expenditures for environmental protection is added to that for protection of human resources, the figure becomes significant.

Affirmative Action

The second major focus of societal concern and resulting federal legislation was in the area of ending job discrimination and equalizing access in the job market. Women and members of racial and religious minorities have often been denied jobs and promotions because of their status. The civil rights movement of the 1960s and the women's rights movement of the 1970s have done much to sensitize America to the inequalities in terms of both employment opportunities and income distribution within our society. Remedial legislation that attempted to end discrimination is surely an important landmark in our social history.

Unfortunately, a great deal of dissension has been brought about by the way in which this legislative intent has been implemented. A mass of laws, executive orders, federal guidelines, and court decisions affects almost every aspect of economic and social relationships; combined, they make discrimination by race, color, sex, religion, age, or national origin illegal.

The Equal Employment Opportunity Commission (EEOC), formed originally under the Civil Rights Act of 1964, was given powers to investigate, negotiate, and publicize discriminatory practices. The mandate of the act was changed in 1972 to give government the authority to sue employers and organizations when it felt that discrimination had taken place. Under the 1972 legislation, the burden of proof lies not with government but with the employer to prove that he is not discriminating. It is not enough to show that practices that lead to job discrimination have ended; results in terms of who was hired or promoted must be given. The power of the EEOC was made clear by the Supreme Court in the landmark case of *Griggs* v. *the Duke Power Company*. In its opinion the Court stated that it was the result and consequences of an employer's action that were important, not the employer's intent. When the employer does not measure up to the federal guidelines, positive remedial action to correct past imbalances must be taken.

A second mechanism used to attack the problem of job discrimination has been the use of presidential executive orders. These orders require that any organization doing business with the government must cease discrimination and act affirmatively to correct past abuses. Since 1970 this mechanism has been used to require any organization having more than fifty employees and receiving over $50,000 in federal contracts or grants to submit a written affirmative action program. Both goals and specific timetables must be set to insure that its labor force reflects the statistical characteristics in terms of minorities of its surrounding geographical area. In addition, a rather large record-keeping responsibility detailing recruitment, hiring, compensation, promotion, and disciplinary action must be accepted for each job classification and by sex and race.

Failure to comply with these standards or to meet goals and timetables subjects the offending company to loss of contract. The compliance mechanism under the executive order is a nightmare of bureaucratic bungling. Some fifteen different federal agencies under the coordination of the Office of Federal Contract Compliance (OFCC) monitor the affirmative action program. Each of these agencies has its own set of rules and regulations, which are often in conflict with those of other agencies. While an affirmative action program may be acceptable to one agency, another may require an entirely different format and, therefore, the planning of a wholly different program. Companies with approved affirmative action programs are still susceptible to EEOC lawsuits.

Added to the bureaucratic cost of administering the EEOC and

OFCC regulations is the expense to industry of changing recruiting and testing procedures and the maintenance of detailed reporting and record-keeping systems. Despite precautions, there is the ever-present fear by business that somehow the best efforts might not meet changing and often contradictory guidelines. The threat of a federal suit or investigation is a harrowing one because, win or lose, the legal expenses are enormous. The damage that can be done to a corporation's reputation, even if the suit is successfully defended, may be great. One of the first suits settled was a sex discrimination suit against AT&T. In this case, the telephone company agreed to pay some $75 million to both employees and prospective employees. The 100,000 case backlog of the EEOC at the end of 1974 and the expected 80,000 complaints in 1975 are evidence of the swelling tide of complaints and subsequent costs.

The increased societal concern for the end of discrimination in the hiring and promotion process is a classic case of how a positive societal change can have unintended, even adverse, effects on economic growth. The implementation of affirmative action programs has caused distortion both within the company and in the job market. Expensive recruitment campaigns are undertaken in order to meet a minority quota, not just to get the job done. In certain areas such as engineering, where the pool of qualified black and women applicants is rather small, premium salaries are given in order to meet the goal. There is always the danger that less qualified applicants will receive employment while more qualified applicants lose out just because they happen to be members of a majority, not a minority. The long range effects of affirmative action programs may well be, as their sponsors state, to increase equality and to lead to more efficient use of our human resources. The short run effects have often been the opposite: increased costs without corresponding increases in productivity. Perhaps the increased participation of minorities of all kinds in the economic process will reduce the need for the federal bureaucratic intrusions that now exist. Unfortunately, past experience with federal bureaucracies does not bear out this sanguine conclusion. Once again a justified societal concern has been translated into programs that increase cost and reduce economic growth.

From Buyer Beware to Seller Beware

Many of the same changes in social values that influenced how we viewed human and natural resources and that put limits on the ways they could be used are also responsible for changes in the buyer-seller relationship. At the beginning of the period, American business was relatively free to develop, package, and promote new products with only market-imposed attention given to product quality, reliability, safety, and honesty of its advertising message. Practically, the reigning norm was "buyer beware." By the end of the period, conditions had changed drastically. "Buyer beware" was being replaced by "seller beware," and such terms as "strict product liability," "product recall," "substantiation and corrective advertising," and "cooling-off period" for sales contracts have entered not only the lexicon but the experience of many businessmen.

The early years of this post–World War II quarter century were halcyon times for marketers. The marketing function emerged from the cellar of corporate organizational charts and entered the executive suite. Firms adopted the marketing concept that turned corporate attention from a focus on productive efficiency to the careful study of evolving consumer wants. Technology provided the opportunity and marketing showed the way to the creation of thousands of new and tantalizing products.

Advertising played an extremely important role in stimulating demand for the increasing output of our factories following World War II. However, as American business was selling its products, it was also selling the American Dream. Advertising has been a major force in shaping our value system and with the emergence of television, the tools available to the creative geniuses of Madison Avenue were vastly expanded. Images by the thousands bombarded our collective psyche: Advertisements in print, on the radio, and later on television warned that our attractiveness, success, and happiness depended upon the consumption of some particular product or nostrum. The merchandisers of deodorants, mouthwashes, toothpastes, laxatives, and feminine hygiene products sent the public into fits of collective self-doubt. The ads, the programs, and the magazines in which the ads were carried showed a world that embodied the essence of the American Dream. Appliances and household products were promoted in the setting of attractive dream homes. In this solidly middle class world, happiness and the consumption of the material abundance that America offered were firmly connected by the nexus of advertising. In this sense the promotional aspect of marketing programs became social change campaigns.

Marketing success has contributed to the rising tide of consumerism. Product choice exploded over the twenty-five-year rocket ride as marketers created products satisfying needs of all types of users. Simple products such as soap, ice cream, and facial tissues were transformed by eager marketers into a plethora of varying sizes, packages, flavors, colors, textures, and composition. In the automobile industry, the number of models, options, and colors seemed to multiply yearly. Every possible permutation or combination of product that buyers would want was researched and marketed. As buyer options multiplied, however, a feeling emerged on the part of consumers that they were helpless in making informed decisions.

Promotion and advertising have been utilized by marketers to differentiate their products. Advertising stresses brand names and tries to develop impressive product images, often to the exclusion of information on quality and price. Companies want buyers to rely on their reputation as the basis for product choice. Consumers in need of relevant information are often met with only exaggerated claims; misleading terms and labels, pseudoscientific studies, the use of premiums, prizes and contests, and cute brand names. With a more educated populace, there is growing intolerance with such marketing practices and growing resentment toward the day-in and day-out impression created by advertising. The Saturday morning television landscape has children sitting through a panorama of cereal, toy, and fast-food commercials that are designed to establish brand loyalty at a young age. Our children and parents alike are solicited by clever marketers to confuse parental love with the purchase of some toy or cereal.

Another problem with the wondrous products resulting from the joining of technology and marketing is the potential danger of the use of many of them. The adding of a power source to so many products increased not only the speed at which they operated, but also the rapidity with which they can inflict personal injury. The chain saw can be used to fell and cut up a tree in a fraction of the time needed with a manual saw, but it can also mangle a human body in an instant. Similarly, a speedboat can provide a lot of pleasure, but can also cause personal injury or even death. Products have become highly complex as they do so much more for the user. This has made them difficult and costly to repair, and has increased the likelihood of maintenance problems. Indicative of the increasing complexity of products, a modern automobile is assembled from 15,000 parts, double the number of parts going into an automobile produced in the 1940s. There is much more that can go wrong with a car equipped with a standard package of automatic transmission, power steering and brakes, and air conditioning than with a car without these product enhancements. Television is said to be the most complex consumer product ever built and it can be responsible for some sudden and shocking repair bills. All of these consumer problems associated with potential injury from a product and with costly and aggravating repair bills gave support to the growing consumer movement.

Consumerism as a movement, however, languished in the backwaters of public attention for most of the twenty-five-year rocket ride. As material progress increased, so did the complexity of products and of the marketplace; and consumers felt their growing impotence relative to the creative machinery of business. In 1962, President Kennedy articulated this disquietude when he proposed a consumer bill of rights. The concerns of this speech captured much of the mood of consumers and presaged the focus of later legislative actions. Kennedy stated that the consumer had the right to be informed, be safe, have a choice, and be listened to on the goods and services that he bought. Initially, the responsibility for consumer protection was divided among, if not necessarily shared by, some twenty-three different federal agencies. Under President Johnson, the concern that Kennedy had expressed was institutionalized under the auspices of a special assistant to the president for consumer affairs.

A major milestone on the road to change from "buyer beware" to "seller beware" occurred with the emergence of Ralph Nader as a leader in the consumerism movement. Nader charged that GM's highly successful Corvair was "unsafe at any speed." He proved his contention in the only court that was important—the court of public opinion; the Corvair disappeared from the marketplace. His victory gave consumerists and, more importantly, the consumer movement a shot in the arm and led directly to the passage of the Automobile Safety Act of 1966. This act became the first installment, the vanguard of consumer legislation in such diverse areas as fair packaging and labeling, truth in lending, toy safety, cigarette packaging and labeling, and consumer product safety. The increase in such legislation is demonstrated in Figure 3.1.

This legislation is a manifestation of the value changes that were occurring in society. Consumers as voters were reordering the rules of the marketplace, and the courts were quick to respond to the national mood. The new legislation and the legal interpretations that they brought forth led to such doctrines as strict liability. It was no longer adequate for a manufacturer to prove that his product was safe if used according to the directions. Under new standards, the manufacturer was required to design a product to protect the user even if he used the product improperly.

The legislation passed during this period changed the way American business sold its goods. One of the foremost areas of change related to product safety. Strict standards were applied. If even a small percentage of a product was found to be potentially dangerous, recall was required. In all, the product safety acts gave seven federal agencies, led by the Product Safety Commission, the authority to recall unsafe products. In 1974, over twenty-five million items were recalled at huge cost both in money terms and to the reputation of the firms involved. The new legislative initiatives and the changing environment of buyer-seller relations are mirrored in the number and amount of product liability lawsuits. In recent years over half a million such suits have been filed, many using the legal device of a class action.

The second major thrust of the consumerist movement has been a frontal attack on promotion practices, prominently the advertising field. After a long period of lassitude, the Federal Trade Commission—under pressure from the Naderites, a newly energetic American Bar Association, and enraged consumer advocates in Congress—began to crack down on advertising. Manufacturers were required to substantiate their marketing claims. In cases of blatant distortion, companies were required to buy advertising that corrected past misrepresentations, in sharp contrast to the more laissez faire days when it took the FTC twelve years to take "liver" out of Carter's Little Liver Pills.

Special legislative and legal attention was given to certain industries and products. The frequency and content of advertising on children's shows came in for special attention, as did the nature of this type of show itself. Cigarette advertising was banned from radio and television, and the FTC required a health warning not only on each pack and carton but in each ad in the print media. The Fair Packaging and Labeling Act required more information on product quality and ingredients. It severely crimped and restricted many of the superlatives, slogans, and pictures that had been used to move the product. Gone forever were the big gallon and the permanent "cents off" promotions. In the big ticket items sold door-to-door such as encyclopedias and vacuum cleaners, a three day cooling off period was introduced. The Truth in Lending Bill required that both the amount and rate of interest be given the consumer in large print.

This new legislation is having a dramatic effect on both the legalities and the morality of the marketplace. Certainly, many existing wrongs have been addressed, and some attempts have been made to correct them. Safer products are surely a public good; any increase in the information and decrease in the deception of advertising and packaging would be useful. But just as in the case of spreading concern for natural and human resources, the consumerist legislation has imposed an economic cost that will be ultimately borne by consumers in the price they pay for goods and services. This cost is both tangible and intangible. The tangible costs are incurred by businesses over a broad area from the design of products to their end use by the public. The time and effort needed to design a product to be idiot-proof costs more than to design one that would normally be safe if used properly. The manufacturer, bringing a new product to market or even promoting an existing one, must not only meet the test of the marketplace but must also run the gamut of consumer watchdog agencies, notably the Product Safety Commission. In promoting the effectiveness or desirability of their products, business must substantiate all advertising claims. If it is not able to, the offending company may be forced to run costly corrective ads under the watchful eye of the Federal Trade Commission. If a product proves to be defective in use, an expensive recall may be ordered. The company involved not only pays for the repair or replacement but also for the intangible damage done to the image of their products. Since the passage of the Motor Vehicle Safety Act, over forty million cars have been recalled; and in 1973 such a large number of automobile recalls were issued that they exceeded production that year. A dangerous or misused product resulting in personal injury to a consumer may mean a costly legal defense in a product liability suit. The addition of a consumer affairs office to the majority of large corporations has increased the administrative cost of doing business.

The net result of the changing social values and the new marketing environment that they beget has been to increase the cost and decrease the speed of introducing new products. Business may deserve in part some of this regulation—they should have policed their own marketing practices better. But it should be understood that consumer legislation has economic costs, which when combined with similar costs for environmental and human resource programs, mean that society is using its scarce resources not to have more, but hopefully to have better. Whether it is getting its money's worth from these expenditures is a moot point. That the bargain is being struck is no longer deniable.

Conclusions

Much of our discussion of the effect of changing societal values has been in terms of recounting the laws, important in and of themselves, passed in such areas as the environment, human resources, and market practices, and the pattern to be observed in each of these areas. During the middle and late 1960s and early 1970s, hallmark legislation was passed, often followed by a period in which a new bureaucracy was constructed. The full impact of the legislation is only now being felt, and in some cases the legislative machinery set into motion in the late 1960s and early 1970s will only have its fullest effect on the economy in future years.

Equally as important as the legislation itself are the underlying changes in the way society views its problems and what it expects government to do about them. Society has increasingly communicated through its political process that it is willing, and indeed wants, to have a larger share of its resources devoted to solving problems of the environment and human resources and to correcting marketing practices. Implicitly, it is agreeing that it is willing to pay the price for these commitments by investing a smaller proportion of its present resources in the future production of goods and services. Unfortunately, the costs implicit in this bargain have often been de-emphasized. Proponents of remedial legislation in these areas have often left us with the impression that we can clean up the environment, right the wrongs of discrimination, and restructure the buyer-seller relationship at little or no cost. Any society has the right and indeed the duty to determine how its resources should be allocated. This decision, however, should be a reasoned one.

It is time that the full economic impact of recent legislation embodying social change be presented in realistic terms. This required movement should go beyond the simplistic pronouncements of the zero economic growth groups, environmental purists, and professional consumerists, and the equally shrill counterchorus of their arch-conservative opponents. The question that needs to be asked is not one of whether or not we want a clean environment, but of what price we are willing to pay for what degree of cleanliness. What is the tradeoff between economic growth and environmental protection? In the area of equal employment rights, the question should be one of how we can end discrimination without reimposing a reverse discrimination, which has been a counterproductive tendency of EEOC. In the area of buyer-seller relations, great care must be taken to insure that in trying to regulate every aspect of this relationship we don't reduce the capacity of the seller to merchandise his product.

A series of laws, regulations, and other manifestations of societal change in the later 1960s and early 1970s have increased the cost of doing business, increased competition for scarce capital resources in many cases, and inhibited normal business practices in others. The effect of these forces has been to reduce our capacity to produce more goods and services. This, unfortunately, occurred at the same time that our storehouse of economic innovations had diminished and when plentiful and cheap energy resources were no longer available. In isolation, changes in social values and the resulting legislative changes would have had significant impact upon the economy. In concert with decreased innovation and increased energy costs, the implications of these changes in societal values become much more serious: the convergence of these forces magnifies their individual impact.

chapter four

The Innovation of the Century

The brightest cluster of forces responsible for our economic momentum since World War II is the growth industries. Each of these explosive industries is based upon the exploitation of a technology. As technologically superior products are developed and marketed, they act as economic catalysts: capital investment is attracted into these growth industries as a result of the attractive profit opportunity that exists; new plants and equipment must be built; and manufacturing and marketing operations must be begun to produce the innovative product. These activities mean new jobs, more income, greater purchasing power, and a resulting stimulation to the economy.

When several innovations are being launched and developed simultaneously, they together propel an economy to greater levels of economic growth. The profusion of technologically superior products developed following World War II united to keep the economy functioning at high levels over most of the twenty-five-year rocket ride. In the following two chapters, several of the major growth industries will be examined. What will be revealed is that many of the key growth industries have slowed down and are maturing at about the same time. While technological advances continue to be made and innovative products introduced, they do not come close to matching the impact of the earlier breakthrough technologies. The loss of technological thrust is dragging heavily on the economy.

Motorization

The most important economic innovation of the century has been the automobile. It was responsible for much of the economic fervor during the Roaring Twenties. From 1930 to 1945, the upward thrust provided by the automobile industry was blunted first by worldwide depression and later by war. The return to peace following World War II allowed the automobile to be developed to its fullest extent. As the adoption of the motor car became widespread, its economic impact was immense and extended over much of the twenty-five-year rocket ride. It became the dominant mode of personal travel and thus had a transforming effect on society. Where people lived, the nature and location of their work, and how they relaxed were all affected by the coming of the automobile era.

Like a stone thrown into a pond, the development of the private motor vehicle set off waves of private and public expenditure in secondary industries that helped feed the tweny-five-year rocket ride. As the population increasingly gained the personal mobility of the automobile, city dwellers flowed into the suburbs. This induced massive investments in single family homes, in extensive road systems moving traffic from the central city to its outer living ring, in shopping facilities to serve the growing throng of suburbanites, and in construction of new and efficient manufacturing and wholesaling operations.

One of the most important effects of the automobile was to open suburban frontiers, but now suburbia is no longer a frontier land and has limited potential for further exploitation. The American Dream of the spacious home in the suburbs, away from crime, congestion, and industrial pollution, and where the cost of public services was low, is tarnished. Furthermore, the public's enchantment with the automobile has faded. These new realities are ominous soundings for the future stimulation of economic growth by the innovation of the century. This section will explore the processes set into motion by the automobile that are now grinding to a halt.

Automobile from 1900 to 1945

At the turn of the twentieth century, the motor car was an unreliable luxury product, more novel than functional. The history of the automobile as a mass phenomenon began in 1914 with the completion of Henry Ford's assembly line for producing the "Model T". The price of an automobile was reduced to a level affordable by millions. The quality of automobiles was also improving. The crank starter was replaced by the electric starter, and the canvas top, open touring car evolved into the hardtop, closed-in model. Body style became longer and lower as the roads improved. These steps made the automobile safer and more maneuverable. With the decline in price and the improvement in quality, automobile sales soared from around 600,000 in 1914 to 4.5 million in 1929 (see Figure 4.1). Total car registration climbed from a few thousand in

FIGURE 4.1: Annual Automobile Factory Sales

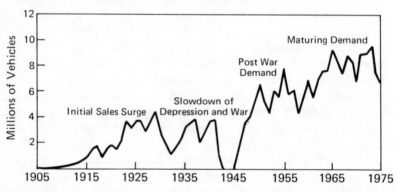

Source: Automotive Industry, *Annual Statistical Issue.* Used by permission.

FIGURE 4.2: Passenger Car Registrations in the United States

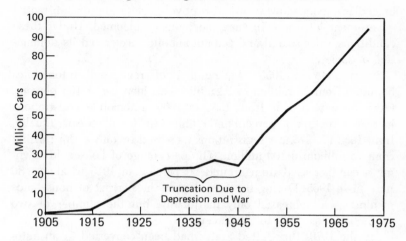

Source: U.S. Department of Transportation, Motor Vehicle Manufacturers Association 1971 and 1972 Automobile Facts and Figures. Used by permission.

1900 to 23 million in 1929 (see Figure 4.2), at which time there was one car for every five people.

The automobile roared out of the 1920s into sixteen years of silence. The Great Depression and World War II postponed the ongoing expansion of the automobile until 1946. High levels of unemployment and falling incomes of those still employed cut demand for cars during the 1930s. Thirty-one million cars were produced between 1920 and 1929, while production reached only 25 million cars during the decade of the Depression. From 1942 to 1945, the production of civilian cars was banned as factories turned to the munitions of war. Production of automobiles did not exceed the 1929 level for 20 years. The temporary truncation of sales is revealed by automobile registrations, which were only 10 percent higher in 1945 than in 1929 (see Figure 4.2).

Post–World War II Automobile Industry

As the war ended in 1945, the automobile manufacturers retooled for peacetime production. During most of the twenty-five-year rocket ride, the automobile industry did not experience prolonged economic downturns, disruptive world wars, or substantial government intrusion. In turn the industry bloomed. Under these conditions, sales soared and the automobile accelerated its domination of society.

From 1945 to 1955, the number of registered automobiles bounded from 25 million to 52 million—an increase of 108 percent. Over the next decade from 1955 to 1965, automobile registrations increased another 50 percent and climbed to 75 million cars. Finally, from 1965 to 1975, car registrations increased by only a third, rising from 75 million to 100 million. The percentage of households owning a car increased from around 50 percent in 1945 to almost 80 percent in 1965. During the next decade the percent of households owning a car increased only marginally, but the number of two car households grew to 30 percent.

By the 1970s the United States had been converted to an automobile-dominated society. For the trip to work or to the shopping center, for vacations at the beaches or in the mountains, or for taking the kids to school or going out to dinner, the car had become indispensable. More dramatic, though a more subtle consequence of motorization, was the transformation of our cities into sprawling, urban areas. Numerous suburban communities were developed that were tied to the cities by freeways and automobiles. As the American society chose to develop the automobile over other forms of transportation, government expenditures were channeled in support of highway development and away from public transportation projects. Indicative of our total dependence on the automobile is a recent survey showing that only 4 percent of the trips made into cities were by mass transit, compared with 91 percent by automobile.

The automobile has had a broad-based impact on the U.S. economy. It is estimated that the industry directly and indirectly supports one out of six American workers. In 1973, automotive related purchases took 20 cents of every dollar spent by consumers, and purchases of automobiles accounted for 59 percent of all expenditures on durable goods. The pervasiveness of the automobile industry on the U.S. economy is highlighted by its importance to the output of the primary industries. For example, over 20 percent of steel production, over half of petroleum refining output, and two-thirds of rubber production go to the automobile industry. An array of supporting industries has grown up to cater to our automobile-dominated society. These include hundreds of thousands of gas stations, the huge motel business, vacation centers, fast food restaurants, drive-in banks, shopping centers, and so forth.

Merchandising the Car

In 1946 and 1947 Detroit produced basically the same motor car sold before the war. After satisfying the immediate pent-up demand, the auto manufacturers turned to making incremental improvements in the basic technology of the car to enlarge the market demand. These changes were incorporated in the annual model changes that brought about a gradual evolution in the car. Styling and appearance were reshaped, a greater variety of types of cars was introduced, and the car was made easier to drive and more comfortable. These were the methods of modern marketing.

The ten year surge in automobile sales from 1946 to 1955 (see Figure 4–1) was in part a catch-up demand resulting from the low levels of car sales from 1930 to 1945. But the return to the annual model change and sleeker styling also had a stimulating effect on sales. The newer models brought more powerful cars: the V-8 replaced the six cylinder engine; and the automatic transmission replaced the manual shift, so that by 1955 three-fourths of the new cars were so equipped. Over the ensuing years more and more accessories were added to the basic car to make driving easier and to enhance passenger comfort. For example, power brakes increased from 25 percent of cars in 1956 to 56 percent by 1970; power steering increased from 27 percent to 81 percent; and air conditioning increased from 3 percent to 71 percent (see Figure 4.3).

Demand for automobiles was heightened by a proliferation of models from which to choose. The number, type, and body styles multiplied; the standard cars were joined by sports models, station wagons, and compacts, each in several price ranges. Chevrolet had one model to offer in 1946, but by 1970 there were nine models, ranging from the Nova to the top of the line Impala sedan and the high performance Corvette. The market was divided into segments,

FIGURE 4.3: Increase in Auto Accessories

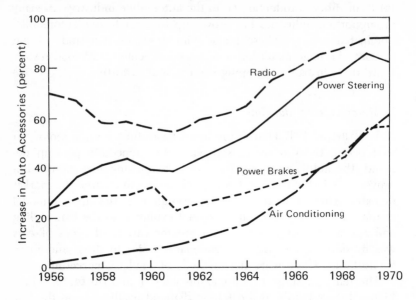

Source: Automotive Industry, *Annual Statistical Issue,* 1971. Used by permission.

each with certain unique characteristics. By the end of the 1960s a customer could buy an automobile that matched his self-image. Variety was further heightened by the availability of an array of options.

The Turning Point

For most of the twenty-five-year period, the automobile industry was unhampered by serious government regulation. Manufacturers were permitted to develop the innovation to its fullest extent, and the United States was converted to a society on wheels. However, beginning in the latter 1960s and extending into the early 1970s, several obstacles surfaced that have adversely affected the use of the automobile and its future growth.

One of the first problems was unfavorable publicity over the safety of the automobile. Ralph Nader's book, *Unsafe at Any Speed,* was not only the kiss of death for the Corvair but also the stimulus for strict safety legislation. Manufacturers were required to equip cars with seat belts, collapsible steering wheels, reinforced steel doors, padded dashboard and visors, and shock-absorbing bumpers. In addition, the industry was compelled to make massive product recalls even when the possibility that injury might occur existed in only an infinitesimal number of instances.

In 1973 and 1974, at the same time manufacturers were changing cars to meet safety standards, the costs of clean air legislation became apparent. The automobile, a primary air polluter, contributed upwards of 50 percent of the air pollution in major cities. As a result, pollution standards were passed that required a 90 percent reduction in new car exhaust emissions by 1975. Toward this end, pollution control devices and the catalytic convertor were added to the car in an attempt to clean up the inherently "dirty" internal combustion engine. Refiners and retailers were required to make costly changes in their operations in order to manufacture and sell unleaded gasoline.

The federal safety and pollution laws required changes in the automobile that increased weight, lowered fuel efficiency, and hiked prices. The mandated changes, coupled with a general price inflation, were largely responsible for the string of price increases that added $500 to 1974 model cars and that led to the second increase of $450, or almost 9 percent, when the 1975 models were introduced. Although in the long run these changes may redound to the benefit of society, safety and pollution controls are not effective marketing tools like styling and optional equipment. Most individuals find it difficult to perceive any tangible benefit from the costly changes that the laws required. The auto buyer knows he is paying more for a less attractive product. A sluggish, fuel-voracious car equipped with an interlocking seat belt device was perceived by many customers to be less attractive than the older model cars.

The sudden tightening of the supply of gasoline in 1973 and its subsequent escalation in price was another blow to the automobile industry. America's infatuation with bigger and more powerful automobiles would never have happened without cheap fuel. While gas economy decreased from fifteen miles per gallon in 1950 to 13.6

miles per gallon in 1970, the price of a gallon of gas increased only 33 per cent, from 27 cents to 36 cents (much of this was due to taxes). Since then the price of gasoline has soared to over 60 cents per gallon, and there is talk and fear of gasoline costing a dollar a gallon in the foreseeable future. This sudden and rapid escalation in the price of gasoline is threatening the future of the big, roomy, luxurious, and heavily equipped car.

America's love affair with the automobile has been stung by both increases in the ticket price of the car and the expense of operating it. The public, now financially strapped, has shifted to purchasing lower-priced models with better gas mileage. Purchases of small cars, which include compacts and subcompact models, jumped from 27 percent to 48 percent of the total car sales from 1969 to 1975. In 1975 the more economically operating imported cars captured a record 20 percent of the U.S. car market.

Once brashly dominant in American business, Detroit is now on the defensive. The president of General Motors says the car of the future must be primarily "functional" and "fuel-efficient." The Omnibus Energy Act of 1976 mandated that automobiles achieve an average fuel efficiency of 27.5 miles per gallon by 1985. Toward this end, GM and Ford together will spend over $6 billion in the latter part of the 1970s on research and engineering to cut the size and weight of their cars. Part of these capital investments will be used to introduce new compact and subcompact models as replacements for existing larger model cars. Earlier compacts such as the Gremlin, Pacer, Vega, Pinto, Valiant, and Dart have been joined by GM's subcompact Chevette and Ford's Mercury Bobcat. Chrysler's large Imperial and Chevrolet's Bel-Air and intermediate Chevelle have been dropped.

The public will buy smaller, less luxurious cars and will make choices from fewer models with fewer options. Styling will be subordinated to function and fuel economy will increase, but then so will gasoline prices. If the cost of gasoline increases faster than fuel economy, operating costs will continue to climb. As the automobile becomes more of an economic burden, growth in sales and use will continue to suffer. Fewer trips around town, car pooling, shorter distances on vacations, and fewer weekend excursions are but a few of the cutbacks that will be made. The frequent practice of trading in cars every three years, especially as models become more standardized and less style oriented, will diminish. The salient question to ask about the automobile industry is not at what rate will it grow, but whether it will move into secular decline. The automobile industry is maturing and growth in production has already stopped (see Figure 4.4).

By the 1970s the automobile, the innovation of this century, was 75 years old. Its acceptance over the twenty-five-year rocket ride has been spectacular, with car registrations quadrupling from the end of World War II to the early 1970s. The period of unbridled development and growth in use of the automobile has, however, come to an end. This has occurred due to public and government concern for safety, pollution, and fuel economy. In addition, the 100 million cars on the road have created a level of congestion making automobile operation difficult. The honeymoon era of the automobile is over. As this phase in the development of our econ-

FIGURE 4.4: Annual Production of Automobiles

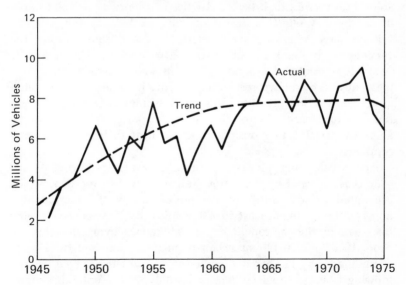

Source: Automotive Industry, *Annual Statistical Issue*. Used by permission.

omy occurs, industrial activity loses one of its most important propelling forces. The constriction on the automobile industry will not only directly hurt car sales, employment, and income, but will also have a negative effect on many of the industries spawned by the motorization of society. The problems surfacing in some of these related industries will be explored in the remainder of this chapter.

Suburbanization

The secondary consequences of motorization have been more important to the economy than its primary effects. One of the most significant consequences of motorization was the opening of the *Suburban Frontier*. Development of this frontier was particularly rapid following World War II as motor cars and trucks became the dominant mode of transportation. The successful conquest of the suburbs was extremely invigorating to the economy.

Cheap land at the city's perimeter could be exploited by the automobile and commercial truck. Families and businesses were able to restructure their basic activities in a more attractive manner by taking advantage of the abundance of land in the suburbs. Middle class Americans could work, live, and shop beyond the confines of the mass transit system. The American Dream of the "good life," centered around a large, privately owned home in a pleasant and attractive residential setting, became a reality. Similarly, motorization permitted businesses to move out from the central hub of the city. With efficient truck transportation it was no longer imperative that businesses locate near their customers and suppliers.

The accelerating process of suburbanization following World War II is reflected in population statistics. In 1940 the central city accounted for two-thirds of the population of the metropolitan areas (cities having at least 50,000 people). By 1970, however, more than half of the metropolitan population was living in suburbia. From 1950 to 1970 the suburban population increased from 36 to 76 million, or by 111 percent, while the central cities lagged behind, growing from 43 to 64 million, or by only 49 percent. The migration of jobs to the suburbs replicates this pattern.

The outward movement of people and businesses created demand for new houses, roads, shopping facilities, industrial parks, and office complexes. These activities complementary to motorization were extremely stimulating to the economy over most of the twenty-five-year period. Unfortunately, the quick and ready abundance of the suburbs has been exploited. Future development will be slower and more expensive. The suburb, no longer a frontier, is maturing.

Postwar Housing Boom

Conditions were extremely favorable for a housing boom at the end of the war. For the previous 17 years, the housing industry had been in the doldrums. So little new construction had been undertaken that by the end of World War II there was a large, pent-up demand for housing just as there had been for cars. The postwar baby boom also added to the demand for new housing in surroundings suitable for raising children. Forced savings accumulated during the war helped families to meet the down payment requirements on new homes.

Public policy actively fostered the housing boom. The Federal Home Loan Bank, established in 1934, helped maintain an adequate flow of funds into savings and loan associations that specialized in making conventional home loans. Through insured mortgage programs, the Federal Housing Administration and the Veterans Administration established the creditworthiness of millions of people who could not qualify for a conventional loan. Interest rates were held down by the policies of the Federal Reserve and the low interest ceiling limits of FHA- and VA-insured loans. The term of home mortgages was extended from 20 to 30 years. The resulting low interest rates and longer mortgages reduced the financial burden of the monthly house payment and brought homeownership into the realm of possibility for most Americans.

Another reason for the growth in housing was the attractiveness of the suburbs as an area in which to stage the building boom. Residential seclusion was much easier to obtain in the suburbs. Bigger lots increased privacy from neighbors, and the mobility of the automobile permitted building away from jobs and merchants.

The wide open spaces of the suburbs permitted large tract housing developments of which Levittown, Long Island, is the classic example. Using an ingenious twist on the assembly line technique of mass production, Levitt built thousands of very similar homes over endless acres of land. He programmed waves of specialized workers from one group of homes to the next until the homes were completed. The early houses typically contained a combination living-dining room, a few basic appliances such as an oven and a refrigerator, and one and a half baths. The product was within reach of the prospective middle class occupant. The entire housing industry was revolutionized by this brash mass merchandising of the house as if it were a bar of soap.

Housing starts climbed sharply after the war to over one million homes in 1946, in comparison to an average of half a million per year during the war. By 1950 the housing starts reached a rate of two million. As the pent-up demand was satisfied, housing starts for the next two decades leveled off at an average of 1.5 million per year. An important characteristic of the housing development was that for the first fifteen years after the war, more than 80 percent of the housing starts were stand-alone, single family dwellings. The high percentage of single family housing meant a large accompanying demand for carpet, furniture, and appliances to stock the house and for shrubbery, seed, fertilizer, and mowers to beautify and groom the yard.

The composition of new housing changed in the 1960s. Single family detached dwellings declined from 75 percent of housing starts in 1959 to close to 40 percent over the period from 1969 to 1973. Multiple family units (condominiums and apartments) and mobile homes grew from 25 percent to almost 60 percent of the total housing market (see Figure 4.5). Then in 1974 the housing market fell apart. In early 1975 housing starts reached the lowest level since 1946.

The precipitous fall in housing starts and the shift away from single unit, single family houses are not mere accidents of nature. The greatest blow to home building has been rising prices. In the past 10 years the average price of a home has nearly doubled; homeownership has grown out of reach for two-thirds of American households. More grim are the estimates of the Congressional Joint

FIGURE 4.5: The Changing Mix in Home Construction

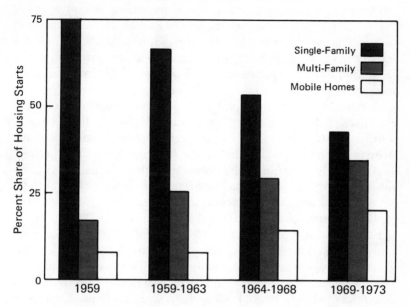

Source: (redrawn from) *Forbes*, November 1, 1974, p. 23. Used by permission.

Economic Committee that claim only 15 percent of today's families can afford to buy a new single family home. The escalating price of homes is the result of spiraling land costs, higher labor and material costs, and the building of bigger and more luxurious homes.

Instead of a quarter acre lot, the larger homes are set on a half acre or a one acre lot. The average size of houses grew from 1,365 square feet in 1963 to 1,560 in 1974. The classic home became the four-bedroom-plus-den, two-car-garage, air conditioned house, custom built in a variety of styles from ranch to Mediterranean. Appliances such as dishwashers, garbage disposals, freezers, and washer-dryers became commonplace.

The second disturbing factor has been the upward trend in interest rates, which accelerated during the tight money markets in 1973 and 1974. Rates of 9.5 to 10.5 percent were two-thirds above their 1968 level. In the early 1950s the median price of a house was around $13,400. With a 5 percent interest rate and a 90 percent mortgage, the monthly payment would have been $65, or approximately 18 percent of the median family income. In sharp contrast, the median priced home in 1975 was $37,800. With a 9 percent interest and a 90 percent mortgage, monthly payments would amount to $247, or approximately 25 percent of the median family income.

A third factor deterring purchase of a single family dwelling is the increasing cost of operating a home. Galloping tax increases, soaring utility bills, increasing property insurance, and more expensive repairs have all added to the total cost of homeownership.

An underlying cause of the economic malaise in the housing industry is the *Vanishing Suburban Frontier.* Following the war, land was plentiful and cheap, taxes were low, and there was little congestion, pollution, and crime. Land that then sold for $500 to $1,000 per acre now costs $5,000 to $10,000 or more. Real estate speculation and the limited availability of prime land have driven up the price. Zoning is now stricter, with communities frowning on small lot, high density homes. While tract homes had historically been built with 5 to 6 lots per acre to hold down the cost, restrictions of not more than 2½ lots per acre have been set in many cases. In addition, builders are increasingly required to construct sewers and roads with curbs and drains, further adding to per unit housing costs.

Another deterrent to suburban homeownership has been the transformation of the suburbs into unplanned cities. The seep of the population to the suburbs soon brought with it the inevitable urban problems of congestion, crime, and pollution—problems that had originally led many people to choose a home in the suburbs over the city. With more public services needed for more people, taxes have accelerated. The land, now more expensive, is being used for homes for the wealthy or used more intensively for apartments and condominiums. Those still seeking the American Dream of the suburban home at a modest price must go to the edge of the urban-suburban sprawl. But the long daily commute in heavy traffic, with increasing gasoline prices and threats of gasoline shortages, clouds that version of the dream. All of these factors have dampened the desire of some to go to the suburbs to "get away from it all."

Proportionally fewer single family homes are being constructed.

When the size of single and multifamily housing is averaged, the units that are now being built have less floor space. This translates into reduced expenditures for furnishings, appliances, and the yard. Cheaper substitutes for housing are being sought by financially marginal households. The mobile home industry boomed when units shipped rose from 103,000 in 1960 to 400,000 in 1970.

There is a shift back to more basic housing in an effort to bring down the price to levels affordable by the middle class. Where possible, lot and house size are being reduced. The luxuries of built-in dishwashers and ovens, garbage disposals, two car garages, and air conditioning—standard in the 1960s—are now expensive options. For example, in order to decrease the cost of the house, one of the nation's largest tract developers reduced lot size from ninety by one hundred feet to sixty by one hundred feet and scaled down both house size and the number of built-in appliances. Another shift, seen in such cities as Boston, Atlanta, and Philadelphia, is the return of interest in urban living. There has been an upswing in the renovation of older homes and offices. Also, demolition of older structures of the city has increased to make way for new high rise condominiums and apartments that attract those disenchanted with the suburbs.

Suburbanization and the booming housing market had a vast and pervasive impact on the economy over much of the twenty-five-year rocket ride. They formed the basis for the affluent American lifestyle and expectations for more and better in the future. A reversal has taken place: the suburbs are no longer the fountain of good living, for in the past few years inflation, congestion, pollution, and the energy crisis moved into the suburbs. No longer do the goals of achievement have the same direction: purchasing habits in turn have changed, and housing, once a vital force in our economy, has lost its momentum. As a culmination of these changes, suburbanization—the prodigy of the automobile—no longer offers its thrust.

Highways

As we became increasingly dependent on automobiles and trucks for transportation, and as urban life pushed steadily into the suburbs, increasing investments were made in new networks of highways. The need to move quickly from central city to suburb and between metropolitan areas motivated the development of the highway system. Expenditures on highways soared from $1.7 billion in 1945 to nearly $21 billion in 1970 (see Figure 4.6).

Prior to 1940, construction of highways followed the original routes traveled by wagons and stage coaches. These early highways followed the natural terrain and went through the center of cities. With the exception of some toll roads in the Northeast where traffic was particularly heavy, high speed, limited access highways were rarely built. The cost to state and local governments of building superhighways was considered to. be prohibitive. Furthermore, the technology of highway construction was in its infancy, and modern methods of road design, construction techniques, and durable materials had yet to be developed.

FIGURE 4.6: Total Highway Expenditures

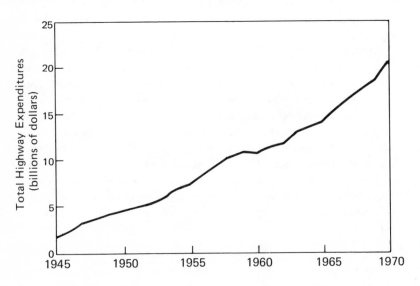

Source: U.S. Federal Highway Administration, *Highway Statistics Summary Manual*, 1966–1975.

During World War II, much of the road system was neglected due to manpower and material shortages. With the return to peace, investment was plowed into upgrading the condition of existing roads. While a few cities built four and six lane parkways from the heart of the city into the suburbs, the major expressway and highway building waited until federal programs were in place.

Congress, realizing the need for an improved highway system, passed the Interstate Act of 1944 which was intended to facilitate the building of a massive network of 41,000 miles of toll free superhighways. The financing of this "super-road" system, however, fell heavily on the states and only 1 percent of the systems were completed by 1956. At the same time, the suburbanization movement strengthened the demand for larger highways to handle the increased traffic.

The Highway Trust Fund was established by the Interstate Defense Highway Act of 1956 and was financed through federal excise taxes on fuel, trucks, cars, tires, and various automotive products. By requiring the federal government to pay 90 percent of the cost of the interstate system, both the burden on the state governments and the major obstacle to the highways' construction were removed. The financial commitment by the federal government underscored the priority given to the motor vehicle. Serious building of the entire interstate system began in the latter part of the 1950s. This vast system promised a free flow of traffic, unhindered by stoplights, from the Rio Grande to the Great Lakes and from the East Coast to the West Coast.

Placing an economic value on these highways would be impossible. Although the expenditures on highways have averaged approximately 2 percent of annual GNP, the effect has been far greater. It is hard to overstate the social and economic impact of the urban expressway and interstate highway systems. The expressways and highways opened the suburban frontier for development and improved the speed and comfort of travel between cities and across the country. The multilane concrete freeways also spawned in their wake a powerful trucking industry, a vitalized tourist business, and a torrent of gas stations.

The social and economic effects of the interstate system are quite noticeable in the pattern of development of urban centers. Initially, highways radiated from the center of the city in spokelike fashion in order to move people to and from the suburbs. Consequently, the space between the city and the suburbs became densely filled by residences, industrial parks, and shopping centers. Largely as a result of interstate highway systems, perimeter beltways were built that enabled travelers to go around, as well as through, cities. Housing, industrial developments, and shopping centers sprang up along these circumferential highways and added to the momentum of the suburban movement.

Today 85 percent of the interstate system is complete and much of what remains may never be built. The cost of the interstate system in metropolitan areas has skyrocketed. Furthermore, social attitudes have shifted as the costs of paving over the landscape—congestion, pollution, and the destruction of neighborhoods—have become apparent. Completion of major sections of the interstate system planned to run through cities is being met by great citizen resistance. Furthermore, the Highway Trust Fund, once exclusively reserved for funding of the interstate system, is currently being appropriated for other types of urban transportation. The reduction of the maximum speed limit to 55 miles per hour and the rapid increase in the price of transportation fuels has dampened interest in completing the superhighway systems.

The problem today is that the economic impact of the highway system has already been felt. The road system of the future is largely in place, and most of its benefits have been realized. It will be hard to come up with a sequel to the stimulation enjoyed from the highway-building boom that has already occurred.

Shopping Facilities

Another significant consequence of motorization and suburbanization was the need to build new shopping facilities to serve the growing numbers of suburban households. Motorization and suburbanization changed not only the location but also the methods of retailing. Innovative merchandising techniques that took advantage of the new suburban locations were introduced and developed, and vast investments were needed to implement these new methods of retailing.

The suburbanization of retailing has meant a movement toward *self-service* and *mass merchandising.* Supermarkets, giant drugstores, and general merchandise discount stores are examples of this phenomenon. These retailers were larger scale operators than their predecessors and were able to sell an assortment of complementary merchandise on a lower cost, self-service basis. High volume and turnover accompanied by lower margins permitted them to sell at lower prices than the traditional service, credit-extending merchants.

The supermarket was invented during the 1930s, but its expansion was retarded by the Great Depression and then by the war. It was not until after the war that its development moved into high gear. The increasing mobility provided by the automobile and the growing suburban population provided the potential needed to sustain large numbers of high volume supermarkets. Also, large tracts of relatively inexpensive land were available for building large, single level stores with big adjacent parking areas. In addition, improvements in refrigeration hastened the acceptance of the supermarket. Spoilage of perishable products was reduced, along with the need for making frequent purchases from nearby food stores. Furthermore, supermarkets offered customers the convenience of broader product lines: They could shop for fresh meat, produce, dairy, bakery, and packaged groceries all at the same store.

An important consequence of the innovative supermarket was the falling cost of distributing and retailing food. The neighborhood food stores operated on a 30 to 35 percent margin. In contrast, the margin of supermarkets is about 20 percent. From self-service, we gained efficiency in the distribution of goods; a greater variety of products was marketed in larger volumes and at lower costs.

Given their price advantage, wider product mix, and more pleasant environment, the supermarkets' share of the market increased from an estimated 20 to 25 percent of food store sales in 1946 to 65 percent in 1960. During this same time span, the number of supermarkets rose from an estimated 5,000 to 23,000. The investment that flowed into this superior method of retailing and its embodiment in shopping facilities contributed to the expanding economy. However, by the early 1960s, the opportunities for continuation of the same high rate of growth in the number of supermarkets had greatly diminished. The market saturation level was approaching, and indicative of this falling opportunity for capital investment was the sharply reduced rate of return on investment earned by the supermarket chains. In the latter half of the 1940s the rate of return averaged close to 18 percent—a very high rate that encouraged investment. By the early 1960s this figure had fallen to around 12 percent (see Figure 4.7). Certainly more investment was to be made in this innovation, but at a slower rate—more closely approximating population growth.

The pioneering of discount stores occurred in the early and mid-1950s when supermarket development was in full swing. While

FIGURE 4.7: Supermarket Sales Versus Return on Investment

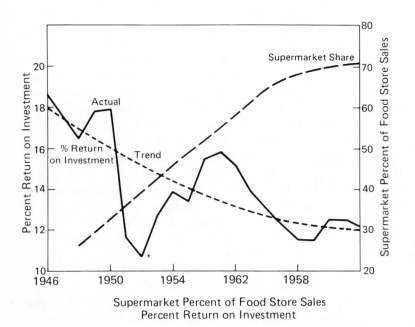

* Depressed returns due to price controls during the Korean War.
Source: Annual Survey Issues of *Supermarket News* and *Progressive Grocer.* Used by permission.

supermarkets specialized in food, discount stores focused on such general merchandise as clothing, sporting goods, appliances, hardware and building materials, automotive supplies, and lawn and garden items.

As discounting came of age, it changed from the club membership approach in low cost, out-of-the-way facilties to open-door discounting in conveniently located new buildings. From the late 1950s to the early 1970s, the number of discount stores tripled, from around 1,500 to almost 5,000. In addition, sales climbed almost tenfold from around $3 billion to $30 billion. By 1972 discount stores accounted for approximately 40 percent of the total sales of general merchandise. Discounters brought down operating margins from the typical 40 percent level of full line department stores to 25 percent.

By the early 1970s the discount store phenomenon had matured. Major markets for discount stores were reaching a saturation level or were overstored, and the growth in discount stores slowed to a crawl. The rate of store closings was almost as large as that of new stores opened. Discounters like the giant K Mart turned attention toward the smaller markets where they built smaller stores. The self-service, mass merchandising revolution was well developed. As it had unfolded during the 1950s and 1960s, the economy had benefited through new jobs, rising income, and more efficient resource use. Now the development of the discount store has climbed to its plateau and its vigorous impact on the economy has ceased.

The growing suburbs created a need for a new arrangement of complementary retail stores designed around mobile, auto-driving shoppers. This opportunity was met by the third major retail innovation of the suburbs—the *Planned Shopping Center*. These centers provided ample, off-street, free parking for automobiles. As centers evolved, they were better arranged, so that shopping at several stores during a single trip became much more convenient.

There was a progression in size and complexity of centers as the suburban population grew after World War II. A large number of stand-alone supermarkets became the anchor stores of the original neighborhood shopping centers. Joining the supermarket were a half dozen other stores, which often included the super drugstore, hardware store, and service establishments such as a barber shop, beauty parlor, and real estate office. The neighborhood center basically sold necessities and fundamental services.

As the suburban population multiplied, the market became large enough to warrant community shopping centers. Anchored by a junior department store or a large variety store, community centers sold general merchandise such as clothing, jewelry, and appliances in addition to more basic items. Commonly these centers would contain from twelve to thirty stores.

Appearing with increasing frequency in the latter 1960s and early 1970s were the giant regional shopping centers. Anchored by one or more major department stores, they included from thirty to over one hundred smaller specialty stores, and the entire ensemble was frequently housed in a climatized mall. Unlike their smaller predecessors, the regionals were carefully planned and used very large areas of space. Indeed, they were frequently built on two levels, with fountains, plants, rest areas, restaurants and other facilities which made shopping a full day's activity. Many regional shopping centers also became the nuclei of entirely planned developments that included hotels, offices, parks, apartments, and condominiums. Development of large numbers of these mammoth centers awaited completion of the perimeter freeways, as the preferred location was near the intersection of an arterial highway and the outer belt (or perimeter) expressways. Such locations could generate enough demand to replicate central city shopping and service variety in a suburban setting.

The total number of neighborhood, community, and regional shopping centers grew rapidly during the 1960s and early 1970s. For example, from 1964 to 1974 they doubled from an estimated 7,500 to 15,000. Shopping centers now command an estimated 44 percent of total retail sales. The growth of shopping centers led to the familiar story of opportunity encouraging investment which creates new jobs and growing income.

Unfortunately, the need for shopping centers has to a large extent been satisfied, and construction of new centers is declining. The problem today is that many suburbs have adequate shopping facilities; others have a surfeit of them. As one retailer put it, if a five year moratorium were placed on shopping center construction, sales volume would reach desirable levels. Time lags of two to four years from the planning to the opening of centers, speculative excesses, and poor business judgment resulted in capacity jumping ahead of demand. Time is now needed to absorb the glut of shopping centers, and the economy will no longer be stimulated by increasing investment in shopping centers or discount stores. The opportunities to expand retail services in the suburbs have neared exhaustion.

Shift of Business and Jobs to Suburbs

Prior to the development of reliable and efficient commercial motor vehicles, central city locations were critical to the operation of many businesses. This was particularly true for companies manufacturing, distributing, and marketing bulky products. The assemblage of many such businesses in one area reduced the cost of moving products between these companies and their final customers. Central locations also afforded easy access to the traditional methods of long distance, heavy freight shipment—railroads and waterways.

The isolation of the suburbs from the businesses and jobs in the city led to the description of the suburbs as "bedroom communities." This dichotomy did not last long after the war, for businesses followed the middle class in discovering the attractiveness of the suburbs. The conquest of the suburban frontier by business was hastened by the increased reliability and hauling capacity of trucks and by the construction of multilane highways to the outskirts of the cities. The building of the extensive interstate highway system in the late 1950s and 1960s further contributed to the decentralizing of business. The expanding use of trucks and trailers that plied the growing expressway system freed businesses from the need to locate at the hub of the older, fixed route methods of transportation. Businesses could settle in the suburbs along a railroad spur and efficiently ship their products throughout urban areas and on to customers located in cities near and far.

After the war, the expanding demand for goods required the

building of new manufacturing plants and distribution warehouses, and it was in the suburbs, where land was relatively cheap, that most of this development occurred. In the central city commercial land was priced by the square foot, while in the suburbs it was sold at so much per acre (acre = 43,560 square feet). Because of the scarcity of land and its high price in cities, businesses had expanded upward with their facilities rather than horizontally, and hence most businesses operated from multiple story buildings. In the suburbs single story buildings were constructed. Sprawling upon the land rather than rising above it, the new facilities were less costly to build since there was no need for elevators, stairs, heavy foundations, and steel to support the frame. More important, the single story factories helped in the organization of highly efficient assembly lines for manufacturing products. Labor-saving, mechanized equipment was employed to move products from the assembly line to storage and to load products for shipment to customers. These continuous flow operations were much more efficient than the interrupted operations in the older, vertical, multistory facilities.

The shift in employment to the suburbs is clearly shown by job statistics. For the twenty year period from 1948 through 1967, total employment in manufacturing for the six largest metropolitan areas located in the North and East (the older cities) declined by 15.4 percent in the central cities, but gained 86.8 percent in the outlying areas. In wholesaling, jobs declined 6.4 percent in the central city but rose 247.6 percent in the suburban areas. The data for the six largest metropolitan areas in the South and West, younger and more automobile-oriented areas than the previous six, reveals a like trend. In manufacturing, jobs grew 91.6 percent in the central cities but a whopping 214 percent in the outer rings; wholesaling employment rose by 29 percent in the central cities and by 242.1 percent in suburban locations.

New office space for businesses also shifted to the suburbs, although not on as massive a scale as in manufacturing and wholesaling. Many businesses elected to establish offices in the suburbs in refuge from the growing disadvantages of the city. Increasing taxes and rent, losses in productivity from commuter problems, a less educated labor pool, and difficulty in attracting middle management to big cities all contributed to the outward movement of offices. In addition, the importance of being in face-to-face contact with the facilities in the city diminished with the technological advances in communication.

The migration of manufacturing, distribution, and office operations to the suburbs provided a major shot in the economic arm over much of the twenty-five-year rocket ride. Huge sums of money were invested in manufacturing plants, distribution centers, and office buildings to replace outmoded central city facilities and to stay abreast of market demand. These investments, creating thousands of new jobs, and billions of dollars of new wealth, fed our growing economy. Furthermore, the building of single story manufacturing and distribution facilities helped business to become more efficient. By substituting cheap land and capital improvements in production and materials handling, industry markedly boosted productivity. This increased efficiency in business operations contributed to the rising standard of living over the twenty-five-year period.

Business has staked out and settled down in suburbia; the accelerating effect on the economy has been realized; and in the future, there will be faint echoes from the boom of business construction in the suburbs. The existing stock of physical plant will be sufficient for the foreseeable future. Factories and warehouses will be built as warranted by the much smaller incremental growth in market demand. There is no new frontier calling for the regeneration of the nation's plants and warehouses. The surge in development has receded. In turn, new construction jobs and new income are disappearing.

The twenty-five years of postwar development of the suburbs have changed the frontier into a maturing territory and with this evolution the suburbs have lost some of their earlier attractiveness to business. More people and more business brought the need for more government, paid for by more taxes. Increasing congestion in the suburbs has interfered with efficient transportation of products. In addition, most of the prime sites near choice labor pools, expressway interchanges, suppliers, and customers have been used up. Restrictive zoning limits the remaining supply of attractive sites and has driven up the price of commercial property to several times its level of the latter 1940s and early 1950s. The suburbs are maturing and the economy is the loser.

Farming

Although motorization is most visible in its twin offspring, the automobile and the suburbs, motorization is also the key to the spectacular postwar success of American agriculture. Output per man hour on the farm increased 6 percent a year on the average over most of the twenty-five-year period from 1945 to 1970. This is a rate of increase double that of manufacturing. The pacesetting growth in farm productivity would be unthinkable without the substitution of inanimate power—the internal combustion engine—for the animate power of man and oxen. By the late 1920s, farm tractors provided the "muscle" for plowing, harrowing, planting, and harvesting. The pace of farm mechanization was slowed by the impoverished condition of the Depression years but accelerated following World War II. The average tractor employed in tilling the fields increased in capacity from 27 horsepower in 1950 to 43 in 1970. Instead of one or two bottom plows, tractors pulled three or four bottom plows when turning under the soil, and the pulling of six or eight bottom plows was not uncommon.

After the war, great strides were made in the harvesting of farm crops by machines. Self-propelled grain combines and corn pickers multiplied the efficiency of human harvesters. The quantity of tomatoes now picked, sorted, and boxed by fifteen workers and one machine once required one hundred workers. Ever enlarging in power and capacity, farm trucks lowered the cost of moving crops from farm to market.

The automation of the barnyard allowed the milkmaid and ranch hand to pass into fable. In today's dairy barn only the cow does not glitter with the sheen of stainless steel. Hand milking and manual handling of milk cans have been replaced by automatic milking machines. The milk is then pumped from storage tanks into delivery trucks for shipment to dairies. Likewise, the mechanical blending and dispensing of feed has transformed the process of fattening cattle. Once a back-breaking manual job, this process is now highly sophisticated and automated.

While mechanization allowed greater yields from less labor, the liberal application of chemicals, hybrid seeds, advanced animal husbandry, and improved farming techniques allowed greater yields from the land. The use of commercial fertilizer, derived primarily from natural gas, increased from 15 million tons in 1946 to over 41 million tons in 1970. The widespread use of pesticides and herbicides cut the amount of cultivation needed and reduced the crop losses due to weeds, rodents, and insects. At the same time, the development of improved seeds produced plants with higher yields.

The mechanization of the farm, along with the other technological advancements in farming and the resulting leaps in productivity, fed the increasing affluence of the nation. Indicative of the progress made in agriculture is the declining size of the farm population. In 1946 almost one out of five people lived and worked on the farm; by 1970 less than one out of 20 people were on the farm. One farm worker in 1946 could supply 14 persons with food; one worker in 1970 could supply 47 people, an increase of 330 percent. During the same period, the value of farm machinery (including motor vehicles) used by the farming sector jumped from $6 billion to $32 billion, an increase of over 500 percent. As a consequence of the increase in farm productivity, labor has been released to work in nonfarm industry to produce other goods and services—an important characteristic of an affluent society.

More food produced by fewer people meant that the urban worker had to dedicate a declining percentage of his income to feeding his family. In 1946, 25.3 percent of personal income went for food, but by 1970 this figure had decreased by one-third to 16.2 percent. The declining percentage of the population on the farm and the falling proportions of income spent on food are both plotted in Figure 4.8.

The proportion of income spent for the purchase of food products took an ominous shift upward in 1973 and 1974 after falling almost continuously since the war (see Figure 4.8). In part, this was a result of the recession that began in late 1973, and of recession-induced cutbacks of nonessential expenditures. But, to a large extent, the increasing proportion of income going toward food purchases is a consequence of the higher prices of critical resources used by farmers. Two of the major raw materials used in agriculture are gasoline (and diesel fuel) and fertilizers. Fuel costs have shot upward and are still rising, and many fertilizers and pesticides are petroleum-based products and hence have risen drastically in

FIGURE 4.8: Percent Farm Population and Personal Income Spent on Food.

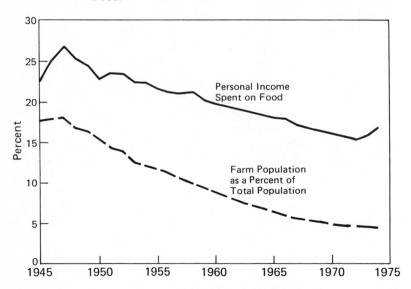

Source: U.S. Department of Commerce, 1975, *Statistical Abstract.*

price. For instance, anhydrous ammonia, the most widely used nitrogen fertilizer, is made with large quantities of natural gas. Since 1970 its price has tripled, from $80 a ton to $265 a ton.

But more important, especially in the long run outlook, are the decreasing gains in productivity in recent years. The annual increase in farm labor productivity of 6 percent a year over most of the twenty-five-year rocket ride decreased in the 1970s to 3 or 4 percent a year and may well fall to an even lower level. The law of diminishing returns has set in on the farm with a vengeance. There are limits to the substitution of machines for human labor and to the application of fertilizer and insecticides to the land. From 1946 to 1970 the population on the farm was reduced from 18 to 5 percent; now the proportion of the population living and working on the farm has approached an irreducible minimum. The easiest applications of productive farm mechanization in the field, in the barnyard operations, and in transporting farm output have been picked. Machines have been customized, specialized, made bigger and more powerful. In fact, they are finally reaching a physical limit to their performance. Tractors that are larger than optimal size are now available.

The practice of dumping larger amounts of fertilizers, pesticides, and herbicides on the land grows less fruitful every year. Biology sets limits to the chemical stimulation of plant yields. While farmers have continued to use more chemicals each year, the yields on major crops such as wheat, corn, soybeans, and other grains have not risen as in the past. What do you do when you have killed most of the weeds and controlled the majority of insects and pests? Technical advancements in improved seed hybrids also seem to have waned. High yielding strains, especially of wheat, corn, and rice, are largely exploited, while other crops, such as soybeans, have resisted attempts to make higher yielding plants. As can be seen, the factors that increased the productivity of the American farm in the past no longer hold the key to future gains.

According to the experts, the major prospect for future gains in productivity is from research into the biological structure of plant and animal life. Hopefully new strains can be developed that will result in larger crop yields and more efficient cattle production. This research for new innovations is expensive and very slow, and impenetrable barriers to breakthroughs may also exist.

In summary, the increasing productivity of the agriculture industry was an extremely important contributor, if not the single most important one, to the rising standard of living from 1946 to 1970. Advances in mechanization and other technological developments, coupled with cheap energy, were the keys to this performance record. But now, many of these product and process innovations are maturing and yielding diminishing returns. Energy costs have shot upward at the same time that technological opportunities on the farm have waned. The consequences are falling gains in productivity and a higher proportion of personal income going for the purchase of food. The farming boom has been disrupted in the 1970s.

chapter five

Waning Storehouse
of Economic Innovation

The great material progress made during the
twenty-five-year rocket ride was to a large extent the result of
technological advances. New and better ways were discovered to
produce an increasing variety of products. Applied technology contributed to a heightened tempo of economic activity through
(1) more efficient production operations, (2) improvements in existing products, and (3) development of new products.

New machinery and processes employed by industry have increased labor productivity, estimated to be from 50 to 90 percent
per worker. The adoption of the oxygen furnace in steel making, the
acceptance of the programmable lathe in metal cutting operations,
and the broad scale use of the computer in office record keeping
have resulted in increased productivity. The introduction of the jet
plane almost overnight tripled the output of flight crews.

Another benefit of technological advances is the development of improved and new products which make life more pleasurable. These innovations create large market demand when the perceived customer benefits are great. The instamatic camera was an overnight success and millions were sold in a few months because customers recognized a significant product improvement. Clothes made from permanent-press fabrics and nonwrinkle doubleknit weaves were quickly accepted in the marketplace for the same reason. The self-defrosting refrigerator was significantly more convenient than earlier models which had to be regularly shut off and defrosted.

Innovative products also create large market demand. For instance, two-hundred-million people now watch television on a daily basis in the comfort of their home; the automatic dishwasher and air conditioning are considered necessities in middle- and upper-income families; businesses would find it difficult to operate today without the computer; and millions are being spent daily on drugs that were developed over the past three decades such as penicillin, tetracycline, tranquilizers, and oral contraceptives.

Major innovations such as television, computers, Xerox photo-copying, etc., create two types of economic activities. In order to produce the product, investment has to be made in plant and equipment. Sales of the product follow after the manufacturing and market effort are undertaken (see Figure 5.1). Additional investment is attracted into an industry when earlier profit expectations are realized. If market demand continues to grow and the innovation is well received, capital will continue to be attracted to the industry to expand capacity. When sales growth levels off as a market matures, the anticipated and real return from capital declines, discouraging further investment.

The "S" shaped sales curve presents a life cycle view of the market acceptance of a new product or service. In the *pioneering* stage of a new product, sales volume is low as final technical problems are being worked out and marketing activities are begun. Next follows a period of *rapid market growth* during which there is broad public acceptance of the product. Often during this stage there are incremental refinements in the product which further enlarges the size of the market. A period of *slow growth* then sets in during which replacement sales increase in importance. *Market maturity* is reached when sales volume is no longer growing and

FIGURE 5.1: Life Cycle of a Major Innovation

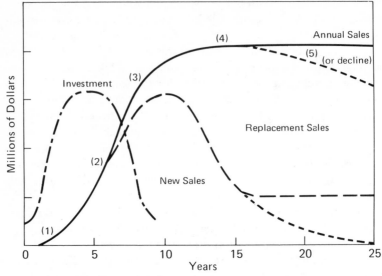

(1) Pioneering (2) Rapid Growth (3) Slow Growth
(4) Maturity (5) Decline

replacement sales are dominant. The final stage of the life cycle, which may occur only after a long period of time, is that of actual *sales decline.*

During the investment stages and period of rapid sales growth of the innovation, new jobs are created which pump purchasing power into the economy. It is in this manner that new products propel the economy. But when market growth slows and maturity sets in, the industry will be hard pressed to maintain current levels of employment. The economy will have lost a source of economic stimulation.

The demand for technologically superior products has not only provided millions of new jobs for the economy but also changed the character of the economy. A dynamic economy is clearly one in which scientific knowledge is being translated into new technology. The continued flow of innovations is of utmost importance for the long-run health of the economy. The twenty-five-year rocket ride was a period supported by major product innovations. The United States entered the period of the 1970s as many of its important innovations were maturing. Unfortunately, they were not being replaced by the new breakthrough advances necessary to generate expansionary waves of investment and employment through the economy.

Developing the Storehouse of Innovations

The seeds of many of the post-World War II technologies such as plastics, transportation, electronics, etc., were discovered in the research laboratories during the decade of the 1920s, including even the very primitive beginning of television technology. Many of these promising technologies had their development and exploitation delayed by the bleak economic conditions of the Great Depression. When existing capital stock in factories, machines, and other tools of production were experiencing low rates of utilization, there was neither the desire nor the financial capacity to invest in new technologies. Furthermore, expenditures on R&D were among the first cost-cutting victims in the desperate struggle by firms to stay alive. The development of new technology and improvements in new products were either shelved completely or significantly retarded.

The beginning of World War II in 1941 snapped the country out of its paralysis by sheer necessity and brought purpose and activity to the economy. Much of the war was waged in the workshops and laboratories of American industries, as much as in the theatres of actual combat. Huge expenditures were poured into R&D programs. Many advances were made in infant technologies that had been largely ignored during the Depression years: New plastics were developed as substitutes for rubber that was in short supply; all weather navigation equipments and skills were perfected; the jet engine was built and jet fuel produced; and the intricacies of the atom were pursued with newly found commitment.

The research establishment which had atrophied during the Depression was resurrected by the war and serviced with vigorous and liberal infusions of government funds. The war proved that R&D could be purposeful and that problems could be solved with commitment of sufficient scientific resources and allocation of sufficient funds. After the war this attitude was translated to firms in their search for profits.

The storehouse of innovation available at the beginning of the twenty-five-year period was large and relatively unexploited and many of them interrupted in midcycle by the 1930s and the war, were now ready to be developed and pursued. New health procedures, food preparation techniques, drugs, management systems, and other war-time innovations were easily modified to the civilian experience. The primary effects resulting from the new advances were increased investment, employment, and output within the immediate industries. Secondary waves of employment and investment were encouraged in industries that directly interacted with the primary industry. As society responded to these new innovations, additional industries enjoyed prosperity, employment increased, and investment grew. The economy was booming and there were good times for most Americans.

Earlier innovations that were incompletely developed because of the exigencies of the period from 1930 to 1945 were fully exploited after the war. Many of the new innovations resulting from the frenetic research effort during the war had, by the end of the twenty-five-year period, progressed to an advanced stage of their life cycle (high on the "S" shaped curve). Although improvements can still be expected in these industries, their major stimulative impact on the economy is now history. Obviously new innovations are still being developed, but unfortunately their impact is much less than that of the growth industries that took off after the war. It is difficult to imagine any future progress to match the economic stimulation resulting from motorization and suburbanization of America, the development of air travel, the revolution created by television, the breakthroughs in pharmaceuticals, the benefits of the Xerox photocopying system, and the growth of computers. In this chapter these innovations will be examined to highlight their importance and to show how their growth has declined.

Television

The development of television following World War II is second only to the automobile as an innovation having a great effect both on society and the economy. Such important innovations occurring infrequently as they do, have a pervasive impact. Before television, the major forms of electronic communication media were the radio and movies. Television combined in a new electronic medium the up-to-date and decentralized information features of the radio and the dual sensory dimension of the movie.

The transforming effect of television can be illustrated by the changes it wrought. The fate of many products and services was tied to the emergence of this blinking, talking, electronic box. The weekly visits to the local movie house where, in addition to the feature, the show included a Movie Tone Newsreel and a cartoon are in large part a thing of the past. Gone are the neighborhood theatres that were centers of community social life. The Saturday morning adventure movies for the kids and the Friday night jackpot are nostalgic memories. Casualties in the motion picture industry were joined by those of other media such as the weekly picture magazines including *Life* and *Look* and the thought-provoking journalism of *The Saturday Evening Post*. Today the average household views nearly six hours of television daily and television has become the substitute in many homes for moviegoing, reading, and even talking.

Television has also had a large impact on what people want and buy. Through what Marshal McLuhan calls the "hot media," businesses in commercial messages not only hawk their wares, but also mold viewers' attitudes toward the benefits of material accumulations. Our material affluence is associated with the repeated interjections of the vision of the "good life" through the commercials we view.

Economic Impact

To appreciate the huge economic impact of television on our economy, consider the following: In 1945 there was no commercial television industry. The mass public had not started shelling out

$500 or more to purchase a television set; there were no television networks developing programs; and there were no local stations with regular broadcast schedules. Today, in contrast, it is unusual to find a home without television. The huge television industry realizes more than $5 billion a year in set receiver sales and repairs, and the broadcasting industry spends an estimated $70 per person annually for a $15 billion total.

To trace the growth of television—the most complex consumer product to be widely owned—two periods can be defined. One begins with the rapid climb in sales of black and white television in the late 1940s; the other with the acceptance of color models in the early 1960s (see Figure 5.2).

FIGURE 5.2: Television Receiver Shipments

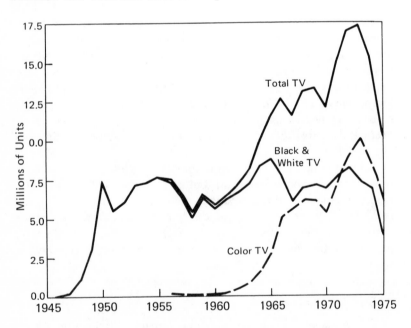

Source: Various issues of *Merchandising Week.* Used by permission.

The first commercial television sets were introduced in 1946, and the early sets were extremely expensive and unreliable, producing a poor quality picture. Production soared from 200,000 sets in 1947 to nearly 1,000,000 sets in 1948 as technological problems were solved and production costs fell. In 1950 seven-and-a-half million televisions were shipped from the factory, setting a record that would not be broken for five years.

In the 1950s unit sales stabilized at a level between 6.5 and 7.5 million sets a year as the period of rapid sales growth came to a close (see Figure 5.2). Actual dollar sales decreased over this period as the less expensive portable and table model sets loomed larger in the product mix. From 1946 to 1960 the number of homes with television sets increased from almost 0 to 90 percent. Three-fourths of the sales by 1960 were for replacement sets. The market was approaching saturation for black and white television sets.

The introduction of color in the late 1950s and early 1960s breathed new life into the television industry—slumping sales of television sets shot up as viewers enthusiastically opted for color television. The vividness of color programming was perceived to be far superior to that of black and white pictures. With color the television industry was again off and running, and the average daily household viewing time increased from five hours in 1960 before color to six hours in the early 1970s.

Much of the pioneering effort in support of the development of color was carried out by RCA, which spent an estimated $120 million to perfect color sets and to start color broadcasting through its NBC subsidiary. Color sets and color programming were first introduced in 1954, but there were a number of problems in the early years of development. Set prices were high at around a thousand dollars, service calls were frequent to adjust and repair sets, and programming was limited. As a consequence, the color television industry didn't flourish until the 1960s when RCA decided to sell their technological know-how to other TV manufacturers who accelerated the marketing effort behind color. ABC and CBS joined NBC in color broadcasting and the number of color programs multiplied. In 1962 a half million sets were sold, compared to only 150,000 the prior year. Sales continued to climb at a rapid rate, reaching five million sets during 1966. From 1966 through 1970 sales ranged between five and six million color sets per year. In the early 1970s, sales rose again but by this time the market had shifted from more profitable consoles to sales of lower priced and more competitive table and portable models. Record sales of color sets were made in the early 1970s, but the profit picture among the industry leaders was dismal.

The increase in color television sales from 150,000 in 1961 to 10 million in 1973 was due in large part to cumulative technological advancements. In 1964 the square picture tube was introduced which made the set less bulky and no longer cut off picture corners. Significant improvements in the brightness of the picture were made with technological advancements introduced in 1965 and 1972. In the late 1960s, automatic fine tuning became popular, and the internal workings of television advanced from vacuum tubes with hand wiring to more reliable solid-state sets assembled with transistors, resistors, and integrated circuits. Screen sizes were expanded from the standard 23-inch set in the early 1960s to a range of screen sizes from 9 inches to 25 inches. Customers were given choices of console, table, or portable models. Furniture styling ranged from the beautiful to the tacky, depending on customer taste and the price they wanted to pay.

The television industry is maturing and virtual market saturation exists (see Figure 5.3). About 60 percent of new set sales are for replacement of older units. The most popular sets today are the less expensive and less profitable table and portable models. Seventy percent of the households have color TVs and the remaining share of the market will be difficult to penetrate. The average color model sells for more than three times black and white sets, and most of the untapped market is resistant to the existing price differential for color. Future sales will depend on replacement needs and new household formation.

Another indication of maturity of this industry is the effort given to product differentiation. Quality, reliable sets are produced in all conceivable screen sizes, cabinetry, models, option packages, price ranges, and in combination with other electronic appliances. Most future technological developments will have only minimal impact on

FIGURE 5.3: Saturation Levels of Black and White TV and Color TV

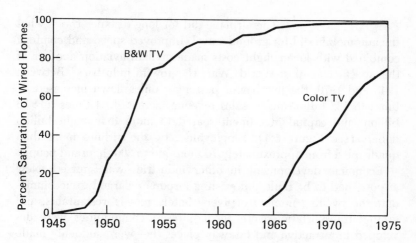

Source: Various issues of *Merchandising Week.* Used by permission.

the market. Competition has turned to fighting for market share and the industry is in the throes of a competitive shakedown. Increasing attention has been given to wringing profits from efficiency in production rather than to product improvement. Certainly there will be continued refinements such as the video disc records and playback systems planned for mass marketing in 1976, but the prices of these changes are going to be quite high and the customer benefits don't appear to be great enough to create a sizable market, at least in the foreseeable future. Cable television, UHF broadcasting, and the like, are expected to expand, but their collective impact is not expected to change the industry rapidly or dramatically. While the prospects for educational television appear excellent, progress to date has been limited primarily by the lack of funding. In its advanced state, television still offers opportunities, but they tend to be either expensive and limited or both. The easy markets for television technology have been captured and never again will the stimulating effects of the rapid growth era of television be experienced.

Airline Industry

The airplane did for long distance travel what the automobile did for ground travel. Improved speed and comfort, combined with lower flight costs made civilian aviation another of the spectacular post-World War II growth industries. Between 1945 and 1970, the number of passenger miles flown increased 37 times to 132 billion miles, sales revenue increased 34 times to $9.3 billion, and capital investment soared to more than eight billion dollars (see Figure 5.4). Employment by the airlines more than quadrupled from approximately 70 thousand to 300 thousand people.

Economic development in other industries was spurred. New airports had to be built and existing airports enlarged to accommodate the swelling number of flyers; hotels, motels, restaurants, and ground transportation were needed; resort communities were developed in attractive and faraway places that were suddenly made easily accessible by air; and the travel agency and tourism business flourished. With the primary and secondary expenditures totaled together, the air travel business contributed mightily to the economy over most of this twenty-five-year period.

The rapid expansion of civilian aviation was a direct result of the huge investment made in aviation during World War II. A major difference in World Wars I and II was that the latter was an *air*-based as well as a land- and sea-based war. When the United States entered the war, it put a huge emphasis on research and development to create an air force. By 1945 with the aid of government expenditures of over $85 billion, the aircraft industry employed over a million people and produced 297,000 planes. From these wartime investments of money and labor came many significant developments that were directly applicable to commercial aviation.

The fantastic growth of the airline business from 1945 through 1970 was the consequence of a series of improvements in aircraft. Technological developments in engine power and airplane design made it possible to fly further and faster, to more airports, and at less cost per mile flown. Changes in the type of aircraft can be observed from the data presented in Figure 5.6. At the end of the war, the two engine DC 3 was the workhorse of the industry. DC 3s carried approximately 20 passengers at 180 miles per hour.

FIGURE 5.4: Growth in Passenger Revenue Miles, Operating Income, Capital Investment

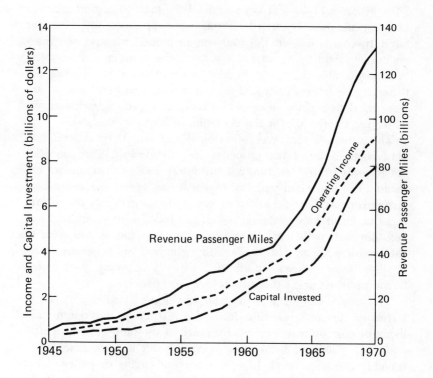

Source: U.S. Civil Aeronautics Board. Used by permission.

The DC 6 and the Constellation were leading examples of the four-engine propeller craft which constituted the first generation of truly postwar civilian planes. They could fly at almost twice the speed and carry four times more passengers than the two-engine planes. Direct flights between most major cities were established as the four-engine planes were put into service.

Turbo prop jets were introduced in the latter 1950s, but were not widely used by the airlines. They were only marginally faster than piston engine planes and mechanical problems impaired acceptance of the turbos. Furthermore, the turbo prop jet was overshadowed by the introduction in 1959 of the long-range pure jet. The Boeing 707 was not only the first but remained the most important member of that generation. It carried 160 passengers at almost 600 miles per hour. In comparison to the four-engine propeller plane, the four-engine jet could fly approximately twice the number of passengers at almost double the speed. Finally, in the mid and latter 1960s the three-engine intermediate range and two-engine short range jets were used to replace most of the remaining propeller driven aircraft (see Figure 5.5, for the evolution of airplane models).

The growth of air travel following World War II breaks into two periods—the eras of the propeller and jet aircraft. The propeller era extends from 1946 through the latter 1950s when the jet era begins. The big initial postwar market for air travel was created by businessmen who could afford to pay a higher price for the advantages of faster long distance travel. Air travel also extended business horizons with local firms expanding to regional and then to nationwide activity. Also the wealthy who had the necessary levels of discretionary income to afford the luxury of flying, contributed to the market during this twenty-five-year period.

The annual rate of growth of air travel is plotted in Figure 5.6. Catch-up demand resulting from the restrictions on nonmilitary flying during the war accounts for much of the high growth in 1946 and 1947, followed by a more normal peacetime increase in air travel from 1948 through 1959, as more four engine propeller planes came into service. The passenger business soared in the early 1950s, and from 1950–53 the annual rate of growth averaged 20 percent. From 1954–60 the average annual rate of growth slowed to 15 percent, and it further decreased to 9 percent from 1957 through 1959. So the market for the quality of air service provided by propeller driven aircraft was maturing.

The age of jet travel started in 1959 when the jets were initially put into service. As more jets were phased into the airline operations, the annual rate of growth of air travel increased from 7 percent in 1961 to 14 percent in 1963, and peaked during 1964–1968 when the annual increase averaged 17 percent. Intermediate- and shorter-range jets replaced most of the slower propeller craft and youth, family, and excursion fares greatly expanded the personal travel market. By the

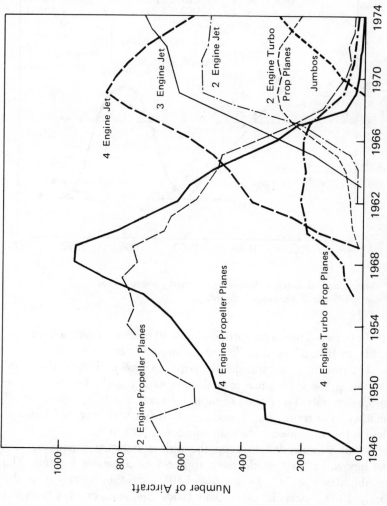

FIGURE 5.5: Number and Type of Aircraft

Source: U.S. Civil Aeronautics Board. Used by permission.

FIGURE 5.6: Annual Rate of Growth in Passenger Revenue Miles *

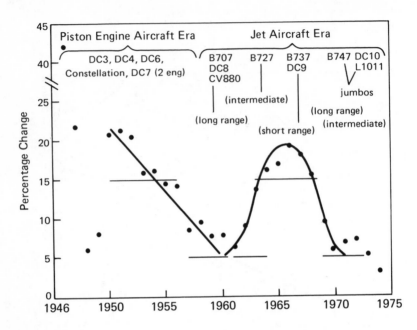

* Data smoothed, using a three-year centered moving average.
Source: U.S. Civil Aeronautics Board.

1970s personal travel comprised almost 40 percent of airline business, up from 10 to 15 percent during the propeller age.

The growth in air travel fell sharply in 1969 and the early 1970s, repeating the experience of a decade earlier with the four engine propeller craft. The period of rapid conversion of the personal travel market from trains, buses, and cars to flying was over and business had fully responded to the advantages of jet travel.

What was needed to keep the airline industry expanding was an innovation that would have appreciable consumer benefits. The jumbo jets—the 747, DC10, and L1011—went into service in the early 1970s, carrying more than twice the number of passengers than the earlier jets. They did not, however, result in significant improvement in passenger service: they flew no faster and were no smoother in flight than existing jets and were not appreciably more efficient to operate. Some passengers even objected to the huge seating capacity and likened their experience to that of flying in a cattlecar.

A competitive drawback of the jumbos was that, because of their huge size, they replaced two or more of the smaller jets. Airlines substituting jumbo jets for smaller planes, reduced the number of flight departures and found that they were losing the important competitive tool of convenient scheduling and sometimes lost business to airlines that continued to fly smaller jets on a more convenient schedule. As a dramatic example of this situation, American and Continental Airlines have disposed of most of their 747 fleet passenger planes and have reverted to smaller capacity planes on more frequent schedules. Acceptable and less costly alternatives to the jumbos existed: several airlines remodeled their smaller jets to have the "wide-body look" of the jumbos. These earlier vintage jets could be remodeled for around $200,000 each compared to the $20 to $30 million needed to purchase a new jumbo. Finally, many of the domestic airlines had placed their orders for 747s in 1967 and 1968 when air travel was growing 15 percent a year. By the time the jets were delivered in the early 1970s, the rate of growth had slowed by half, so that the traffic on many routes could not absorb the sudden surge in seat capacity brought on by the jumbo jets.

There was hope in the late 1960s that the supersonic jet would be an important technological advancement with sufficient customer benefits to rekindle the rate of growth of the airline business. However, the United States government abandoned its research support for this aircraft on several grounds. The SST was evaluated as being an uneconomical airplane that would benefit only a small segment of the population who felt their time was so valuable as to justify the sharply higher cost of flying faster than the speed of sound. Another challenge to the SST was made on the environmental grounds that the SST would be harmful to the ozone layer of the atmosphere, and in turn, have a detrimental long-term effect on our health.

Besides approaching technological and environmental limits on speed, the airline industry is also facing increasing costs per mile flown. Since 1969 the cost per seat mile has shot upward, reversing a downward trend since 1946. A big factor in the rising cost of the airlines is jet fuel which jumped from nearly 11 cents per gallon in 1972 to around 33 cents in mid-1975. This represented an increase in operating costs from 12 percent to 20 percent and further fuel increases are anticipated.

Adding to the increasing cost difficulties of the airlines has been a decline in capacity utilization. For the first half of the twenty-five-year period, the airlines had load factors (percent of available seats filled) in the low 60 percent range. Since then, the load factors steadily declined and fell to less than 50 percent in the early 1970s. There are several reasons for the unused capacity. The Civil Aeronautics Board regulates both prices and routes. The primary competitive tool of the airline industry is schedule convenience, and this has contributed to the airlines' over-buying equipment. Many airlines naively expected to receive new route awards and foolishly overcommitted for expensive new equipment. Finally, the jumbo jets came just at the time when the growth rate of the airlines had been halved. Excess capacity can be used only in due time. Very little new equipment will be needed to meet the growth in the market for several years to come. The industry is now in a capital work-off stage, rather than in an accumulation phase.

The adverse set of conditions confronting the airline industry in the early 1970s included decreasing capacity utilization and increasing operating costs. The slowing rate of growth has led to the widespread recognition that the industry is maturing. Forecasts made in 1975 are for future growth rates of 7 percent per year, which would give increases of 40 percent in five years compared with the recent experience of doubling every five years. With rising fuel costs, the airline industry may not even achieve the 7 percent growth forecast. The economy has lost the stimulation from this once super-growth industry.

The Pharmaceutical Industry

The post-World War II period became known as the "Golden Age of Drug Discovery" and the "Great Drug Therapy Era." It was ushered in by the first of the sulfa drugs in

1935 and by penicillin in 1945. These wonder drugs were the catalysts that created the giant drug firms of today. The industry's growth resulted in a number of new drugs that eradicated many diseases and moderated the effects of many other serious illnesses.

Prior to 1940 most drugs sold by prescription were compounded by the apothecary, who bought the ingredients, measured and mixed them, and put them into capsules. The mortar and pestle were actual tools, rather than symbols, used on a daily basis. World War II changed all this: Millions of men were scattered across the globe, and there was a need for premixed and precapsulated drugs that were easily dispensed. The ethical drug industry met this challenge by mass producing drugs—a major technological development that spurred the growth of the industry.

The problems of disease, infection, pain, and suffering were of utmost national importance during World War II. Starting in 1940 and continuing through 1959 the drug industry, through an accelerated research and development effort, created a constant supply of new products (see Figure 5.7). Through increased knowledge of the human body and disease agents, effective drugs were discovered to treat arthritis, epilepsy, hypertension, allergies, mental illness, and parasitic and infectious diseases. We now have steroids, hormones, enzymes, antidepressants, tranquilizers, oral contraceptives, and a host of antibiotics to sooth, salve, and control the human body. Research also led to improvements in established drugs. Great effort was directed to finding the proper dosage that was most effective and had minimal undesirable side-effects.

The retail sales of prescriptions and over-the-counter (OTC) drugs soared from around 1 billion dollars in 1945 to approximately 9 billion in 1970 (see Figure 5.8). We became a pill-taking society. The average number of prescriptions purchased per person increased from 2.4 in 1950 to 5.4 in 1970. Much of the public felt that there was a pill to cure everything. Because of massive promotions of the drug companies, self diagnosis and treatment also caused a rise in sales of OTC drugs such as aspirin, cold remedies, and digestive aids. But these simple remedies and pain killers did not grow at the same fast rate of prescription drugs (see Figure 5.8).

Besides favorable public attitude, the drug industry had the government on its side in the early part of the era. Strong patent

FIGURE 5.7: New Drugs Marketed Annually

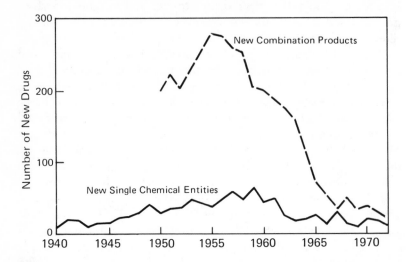

Source: Redrawn from Milton Silverman and Philip R. Lee, *Pills, Profits, and Politics,* p. 38. Used by permission.

laws fostered R&D efforts by giving companies time to earn a larger return on their new drugs. Early government-sponsored health programs seemed in many ways to be tailor-made for the industry. Regulatory standards were not generally considered to be overly strict and enforcement was lax. State laws prohibiting a pharmacist from substituting a different brand of the same drug were passed, as were laws preventing the posting or advertising of drug prices. This reduced the impact of price competition and protected drug company profits.

The public enjoyed great benefits from this era of the wonder drugs. Infant and maternal mortality rates were sharply reduced and average life expectancy was extended. In addition to the eradication of many diseases, recovery from diseases and operations was speedier, less painful, and more complete. The widespread use of vaccination techniques considerably lessened the incidence of such diseases as smallpox, polio, and diphtheria. More effective

FIGURE 5.8: Retail Sales of Prescription and OTC Drugs

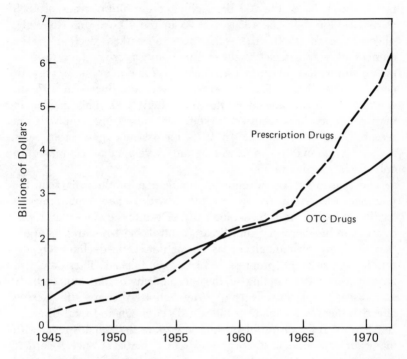

Source: Redrawn from Milton Silverman and Philip R. Lee, *Pills, Profits, and Politics,* p. 213. Used by permission.

anesthetics and germ control increased the potential and safety of surgery. Many ailments could be treated at home with prescription drugs, thus avoiding the burdensome expense of lengthy hospitalization.

Until the 1960s the drug industry had a good press. It was viewed as a partner with the doctor in the preservation of life and as an agent of disease eradication. The payoff to the industry was rapid growth in sales and profit and hope for the future. Since 1960 conditions favorable to rapid sales and profit growth have changed from positive to negative. The lifeblood of the pharmaceutical industry has been a continuous stream of new products. For example, 95 of the 200 best selling prescription drugs of 1969 were introduced in the 1950s and 66 in the 1960s. Unfortunately, since the early 1960s, there has been a marked decline in the number of new drugs (single entities) and a precipitous drop in new combination products (see Figure 5.7). For example, only 16 new drug products (single entities) were introduced in 1970 in contrast to 45 introduced to the market in 1960. This decline in new products has occurred despite an increasing emphasis on research and development. In 1970, almost nine percent of sales revenue was invested in research and development compared to only three percent in 1950.

The reason for the decline of innovative products is that the pharmaceutical industry is now faced with a new environment—legally, socially, and technologically. Despite advances and discoveries in biochemistry and disease control, most researchers argue that there are technological reasons for new drug declines. Opportunities for research progress have not diminished. There are still gaps in the understanding of the mechanisms of the human body and disease and the effects of drug action. We are still lacking effective therapy for many of the world's common and fatal diseases. But current research problems are now more difficult to solve, with many of the easier discoveries already made. Cancer, cardiac impairments, and mental illness syndromes of schizophrenia and senility are more complex and diverse in nature, and the research is correspondingly more extensive and difficult. A major technological breakthrough would be required to develop a really new product.

Much of the increasing cost of research and development efforts has been a product of growing government regulation. Before the 1960s, government control was mainly directed toward certifying the safety of drugs and the proof of their effectiveness in curing or preventing illness was not demanded. The Thalidomide crisis, the Cyclamate ban, and the Hexachlorophene scare have precipitated a strengthening of government control. The industry's pricing policies and production methods have also come under close scrutiny. The drug industry has found itself the subject of a continuing Senate investigation for nearly a decade—twenty-four volumes report highly volatile hearings. Since the enactment of the 1962 Drug Amendments, extensive testing and lengthy procedures are required before certification of a drug takes place. The period required for complete testing and establishment of a new drug has jumped from 2 to 9 years and the time for reaping the rewards of a new product before its patent expires and competition begins has declined. Exemplifying the new problem is the drug, Minocin, which was introduced by the Lederle Division of American Cyanamid after 10 years of an intensive research and development effort at a cost of $7 million. It was estimated that the odds on developing and introducing such a new safe and effective drug through all of the complex steps of R&D was one in 30,000.

The federal government has used its position as a large purchaser of drugs in a detrimental way from the standpoint of the drug companies. It requires that drug purchases under the national health program of Medicare and Medicaid be made at the lowest price of a drug. This action has promoted the increasing use of drugs marketed not by a brand name but by a generic name which allows for an increasing proportion of sales made at lower prices and lower profits for the drug manufacturers.

Traditionally there has been little competition from other drug companies when a patent on a product expires, but now major companies are producing generic drugs which are making inroads into brand name sales. This trend is expected to continue and widen, as more than half of the leading 200 prescriptions lose their patent protection by 1984. Furthermore, the longer time now required to get clearance to market a new drug is reducing the effective period of patent protection. Thus, the growing generic problem to the industry promises to reduce the profitability of the pharmaceutical companies.

Inhibiting the prospects for the pharmaceutical industry's future expansion is its worsening relations with the public. A recent study by one of the nation's top research organizations shows that the public rates the drug industry as number two on the villain scale behind the oil companies. Blamed for soaring prescription prices, the drug industry also faces complaints of untruthful, incomplete, and offensive advertising, lack of product safety, and evasion of government regulation.

There are then many adverse factors bearing on the giants of the drug world. While once the drug industry knew no obstacles to its rapid growth, it now is hampered by technological slow-downs, complex health problems, stiffer competitive tactics, and government restraints. Further government control is expected in pricing, advertising, and production as Senate hearings and other investigations continue. Although growth is still anticipated, it will be harder to realize and is expected to be at a declining rate. The impetus to the economy by yet another high technology industry has been diluted.

Photocopying Industry

Xerography is another innovation that spurred rapid economic growth; in this instance, in the office copier industry. The story of xerography is primarily that of the Xerox Corporation, which in 1960 introduced a new copying technology. From practically base zero in 1960, Xerox grew to control 85 percent of the dry paper copier market and between 60 to 70 percent of the total copying market by the early 1970s. This technology blossomed into a 4.5 billion dollar industry. Xerox's growth had a stimulative effect on the American economy, but unfortunately future prospects for expansion in the industry cannot be expected to equal the frantic pace of the past decade and a half.

Before xerography, the existing methods by which business could make copies of typed materials and documents had a number of drawbacks. For a few copies multiple carbons could be typed or Thermo-fax copies made of the original. Carbon copies were not only hard to prepare, but also difficult to read. Although Thermo-fax copies were easy to prepare, they were of poor quality on a strange-looking brown paper. For larger numbers of copies, wet processes such as Ditto and mimeograph were employed. The short-comings of these processes were that originals were difficult to prepare and the reproduction of copies was a messy job.

The market was ripe for a machine that could produce high quality copies quickly and clearly with a minimum of fuss and bother. The Xerox Corporation produced such a machine when it marketed the Model 914 in 1960. Over twenty years of developmental work preceded the introduction of this dry-paper copier. The Xerox copier is a highly complex machine based on technological principles of photography and electrostatics. The document to be reproduced is photographed and its image is then transferred to a revolving drum. As the drum revolves, powdered ink adheres to the charged surface which is the image to be reproduced. Then a piece of regular bond paper is run over the drum, picking up the pattern of the inked surface. Finally, the dry ink is fused to the paper with heat.

As complicated as this method sounds, the machine was push-button operated and fast, providing good quality reproduction. The Model 914 could produce seven copies a minute and did not require a skilled operator. There were the added features of no contact with any ink or messy chemicals, no waiting for copies to dry, and competitive cost with the more time-consuming processes. The machine was well suited to the requirements of many offices.

Business rapidly responded to the opportunity to purchase Xerox's superior copier, and sales soared. During the 1960s sales doubled every two to three years, and in the decade from 1960 to 1970, Xerox's sales increased an unbelievable 47 times. In dollar volume they rose from $37 million to $2.75 billion (see Figure 5.9). By 1974 sales had doubled again, reaching $3.6 billion. The number of persons employed reflected this sales trend and grew from less than 3,000 employees in 1960 to over 55,000 workers in 1970. By 1974 that number had nearly doubled to 100,000 employees. Indicative of the effect of introducing a technologically superior product has been the unusually high returns on net worth that Xerox earned throughout the 1960s. In 1962, two years after the introduction of the Model 914, the return reached a high of 48 percent, gradually receding to the twenty percent level by the end of the decade. In response to this superior product, stockholder investment (net worth) climbed from $18 million in 1960 to $855 million in 1970 or by almost 50 times. Good investment opportunity (of which the Xerox process is an example) keeps capital investment growing and the economy moving.

Xerox's spectacular growth has resulted from enlarging upon

FIGURE 5.9: Sales of Xerox Corporation

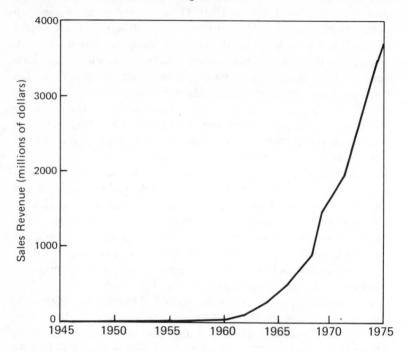

Source: *Value Line.* Used by permission.

the basic technology of the original Model 914 copier. Customers now have a wide range of models that operate at different speeds and with a variety of optional accessories. Following the Model 914, a machine for the medium volume user, Xerox brought out the Model 813, a desk-size copier. Subsequent models were introduced including the Model 3600, 4000, and 9200, which increased the number of copies per minute and added special features. Xerox machines can now reduce large documents, copy both sides, copy color, make 7,200 copies per hour, and collate automatically. The quick copy technology has been applied to serve from the smallest one-man legal office to the largest user in central reproduction centers of large corporations. Xerox now produces a copier for almost every conceivable market and application.

The wide adoption of the Xerox copiers has contributed to improvement in office efficiency and the flow of communication. Secretaries no longer have to struggle with typing and correcting carbon copies. When making a large number of copies, it is no longer necessary to prepare a special ditto or mimeograph master. Multiplication of copies is now just a matter of a flick of the switch. Similarly, the flow of communication has been enhanced by xerography because multiple copies of materials to be distributed are easily and quickly prepared. No longer is it common to receive materials with a buck slip that must be initialed and forwarded to the next person on the list. Everyone involved now receives his own copy of the material at the same time. It was estimated that in 1970, 375 trillion business documents were made, or 1,250 copies for every person in the United States. The general public now benefits from having access to personal use of photocopiers in libraries, shopping centers, office buildings, and the like. For a nickel or dime, one can now obtain a personal copy of almost any document.

Although the copying mania continues and the copiers have become indispensable in business operations, the rate of growth is slowing from that of the 1960s. In 1974 there were 600,000 plain paper copiers of which approximately 580,000 were Xerox models. Nearly every office and organization of any size has a copier or access to one nearby. Most of the potential market has been tapped.

A second reason for a slower rate of growth is that many of the easier applications of xerography technology have been developed. A variety of machine sizes has been introduced for small- and medium-size copying tasks. By increasing speed and lowering cost, more business was developed. Now the newest models are directed at special segments of the market. The size of the market for the costly color copier does not appear great, because most materials to be copied are still in black and white. Another new model from Xerox is the 9200 which was introduced to tap the high-volume copying market. Here Xerox is competing with offset printing and fighting a long-established quality copying technology. Neither the color copier nor the Model 9200 have the transforming potential of the original 914. They are at best incremental improvements and hence cannot reproduce the impact of their original predecessor.

A final indicator of slower growth is Xerox's rate of return on investment. Having reached a peak in 1962, the percentage has slowly returned to a more normal level indicative of a stabilizing industry. In 1974 Xerox showed a profit increase of only 10 percent while the average increase over the prior 6 years had been 16 percent. Xerox's profit actually declined in 1975, breaking a record of 20 years of uninterrupted growth in profitability.*

Obviously Xerox will continue to grow, but at a slower rate than in the past. *Business Week*, in a cover story on Xerox and its chairman C. Peter McColough (April 5, 1976), concluded that:

> The days of booming growth for U.S. plain-paper copier business—and Xerox—are over. In the first half of this decade, the industry's growth rate was 15 percent a year; in the last half McColough expects it to be closer to 8% or 9%.

New jobs and capital investment will not be generated at the same pace. The loss of the expansionary force of this industry will contribute to a slowing down of the growth of our economy.

Computer Industry

The electronic data processing, or computer, industry has been another of the emerging growth areas in the post-World War II period. Growth rates for the industry leader, IBM, reached such heights in the 1950s that, if their rates had continued at the 1950s level, sales of IBM would have exceeded the Gross National Product of the United States by the end of the century.

---

* The loss was largely attributed to the write-off of Xerox's abortive effort to enter the computer business, but was also the result of a slackening sales pace and an increase of competition in the photocopying business.

The computer revolution has transformed the conduct of business and government almost to the extent that the automobile transformed American life.

The rapidly developing computer age has been the result of a fast changing technology coupled with a growing number of applications for electronic data processing. In two decades there have been four generations of development in computer technology. From the vacuum tubes of the early 1950s, computers used transistors by the mid-1950s; by 1965 integrated circuitry was introduced; and by 1971 semiconductor chip technology was common. Each successive step in the innovative process increased the speed, reliability, and capacity of computers to store and process information, and this effectively reduced the cost per computation.

At the same time, a wide range of sizes and specialized peripheral equipment was developed to tap specific market segments. Large main frame computers, "number crunchers" as they are known, have been produced for the scientific research community, universities, and some government applications. Medium-size computers could generally take care of most large corporations' bookkeeping and payroll needs. Increasingly, industrial producers are utilizing smaller computers to monitor and reset production processes. And now the hottest growth market, the minicomputer, is being adopted by many medium- and small-size firms.

The impact of the computer has touched almost every citizen in the United States from the recipient of a computerized bill to the welfare claimant who receives his monthly computer-calculated-and-written check. As with many industrial technologies, the computer is a labor-saving device. One computer can replace hundreds of bookkeepers and do the job with fewer errors. A scientific problem with numerous variables that would have taken thousands of hours of computations can be solved in a matter of seconds. An entire refinery can be monitored from a control panel which would have required the labor of many. The computer has made important contributions to increasing productivity and to improving our standard of living.

As in the photocopying industry, the growth in electronic data processing (EDP) equipment has been phenomenal and led by one firm, International Business Machines (IBM). From an infant industry in the early 1950s, computer sales and service revenues have grown to $20 billion a year by 1974, making the computer industry the fastest growing industry in the United States. IBM has dominated the computer industry, with a 60 percent market share. IBM's sales increased from $142 million in 1945 to $7.5 billion in 1970, an increase of 50 times over. In 1974 IBM had sales of $13 billion and was the second most profitable U.S. company with profits of $2 billion. Its payroll of 300,000 employees makes it the fifth largest U.S. employer.

The growth of IBM and the rest of the computer industry has been spurred by fast rates of technological change that made older computer hardware obsolete. But the technology has now proceeded through four generations. The final advance to semiconductors, while increasing the speed of operations, represents essentially the same computer of the third generation. For many of the most prevalent uses of computers, additional speed and storage capacity will provide only marginal benefits. The quantum jump in speed and reliability and reduction in size and cost, which accompanied the movement through four generations of computers, will be hard to replicate. For example, the cost per 100,000 calculations has fallen from $1.26 in 1952 to $.01 in 1975; a dollar spent on memory today buys 44 times the capacity than it did 23 years ago; and the size of computer memory has been reduced 800-fold over this period. Furthermore, computer companies may be reluctant to introduce new higher speed products that will upset the millions of dollars of equipment they presently rent. When it introduced its faster 370 series in 1971, many of IBM's 360 customers dumped the older machines back on the company which cut into IBM's profits.

One of the cornerstone's of IBM's growth has been its catalog of application programs or, in the jargon of the computer industry, its software. But, after two decades of concentrated effort, most of the ready applications of computers have been met. The major use for computers has been the performance of functions of everyday business and government operations such as bookkeeping and accounting, payrolls and billing, and inventory record keeping and ordering. Computers have long been used by universities, research organizations, and the government to analyze large amounts of data. Even smaller organizations are taking advantage of the computer as evidenced by the rapid growth of both time sharing and the minicomputer market in the last few years.

The growth in new applications for computers has shifted in recent years. According to many experts, "on-line" uses of computers to monitor and direct processes is where the future applications will occur. These applications, which are often extremely complex programs developed for one use or one company, are not easily transferred in the same way that early software packages for payrolls or billing were transferable.

The vast and efficient computer hardware capacity already in existence and the problems of extended applications make it unlikely that the computer industry will sustain its past rate of growth in sales and profits. The giant of the industry, IBM, has experienced a decline in earnings growth from a compound rate of 18 percent over the period from 1964 to 1969 down to 14 percent from 1970 to 1974. Several investment analysts suggest that a growth in the 10 to 12 percent range over the next few years is the most that can be expected. The industry will certainly continue to grow, but likely at a much slower rate than in the 1950s and 1960s.

Summary

At the end of World War II, conditions were uniquely favorable for a rapid and prolonged period of economic growth. The full exploitation of the potentialities associated with the automobile had been truncated first by depression and then by war. With the end of hostilities, the motorization of America and the resulting conquest of the suburban frontier were resumed with renewed vigor. In the process vast pools of labor and capital were employed in changing the nature of the landscape and life style of the American public. By the 1970s the process of conquering the suburbs was basically complete.

The post World War II quarter century was also a period during which many new technologies were introduced. Several of these were spurred by the research associated with the huge war effort. Television, civilian aviation, pharmaceuticals, xerography, and computers were all industries that either introduced new technologies or rapidly transformed existing technologies. They provided investment and job opportunities which supported the economy during the twenty-five-year rocket ride. The market acceptance of these new technologies gave the American economy a force and direction, which allowed it to grow despite the clumsy efforts of both economists and politicians.

The maturing of several of these technologies toward the end of this period has robbed the U.S. economy of much of its growth momentum. No longer can we blithely depend on these industries to provide a back-stop to the economy. When these industries were in their expansion phase, they reinforced each others' economic impact. Unfortunately, as they mature together, they reinforce the movement to slower growth.

Innovations will continue, but it will be hard to come anywhere near realizing the statistical record of the past twenty-five years. It may well take ever increasing inputs of R&D expenditures to get a given amount of economic impact. What do we do for an encore? What will replace the stimulation of motorization and suburbanization of America? Where is the new television, the growth in civilian aviation, and the coming of the computer age? How do we reproduce the investment-producing, job-producing, and life-changing force of these innovations?

chapter six

The End of the Impossible Dream

Cheap and abundant energy was the third of the triad of forces which gave us the twenty-five-year rocket ride. As labor became expensive, we substituted capital for it, and this capital was extremely energy-intensive. The substitution of horsepower for manpower augmented both the productivity of labor and capital and undergirded our rising standard of living. Many of our most important technological innovations in farming, plastics, and transportation for instance, were economically and technically dependent on cheap and abundant energy resources.

The history of the early 1970s shows that the era of cheap and abundant energy is over. The price charged for each of our energy resources has escalated and the pessimists predict that this escalation will continue at the high rates so recently experienced. The optimists hold out, not for a reduction in prices, but for a slowing down of the rate of increase. Underscoring the seriousness of our energy situation was the establishment of the United States Energy Research and Development Administration (ERDA) in January 1975—a supergovernment agency that has as its mandate the de-

105

velopment of lagging energy resources. The chief administrator of ERDA is rather blunt in his warning:

> We are never again going to have a cheap-energy situation, and we have got to use every string in our bow if we are going to maintain the life-style of this country. (John W. Finney, "Focusing On Energy—Unclear," *The New York Times*, March 9, 1975, p. F3.)

The official pessimism of the head of ERDA is echoed in the private sector. For example, an announcement by Exxon, the world's largest energy company, points out the changing energy climate in the United States.

> In basic energy resources, the United States is still way ahead of most industrial nations. . . .
>
> But all these resources will not allow Americans to go on using energy as we have been—at per capita consumption rates double that of Great Britain, and West Germany, and three times that of Japan.
>
> *The age of cheap and abundant energy is over for the United States.* Economic and political security indicate that *energy must be used more efficiently* (emphasis added). (From an advertisement by Exxon in many magazines in early 1975).

The combination of accelerating energy prices, changing societal attitudes towards economic growth, and the waning storehouse of economic innovations is responsible for the end of the twenty-five-year rocket ride.

The high standard of living in the United States is in large part a product of massive energy consumption. This country consumes approximately 35 percent of the world's energy, but has only 6 percent of the world's population. This direct correlation between the growing output of our economy and energy consumption is illustrated for the post-World-War-II period in Figure 6.1. Output of goods and services (GNP) increased 130 percent in real terms from 1946 to 1970, while our consumption of energy increased by 126 percent. Over the same period the average energy use per person in our economy increased by approximately 50 percent. Because the

FIGURE 6.1: Gross National Product Related to Energy Use

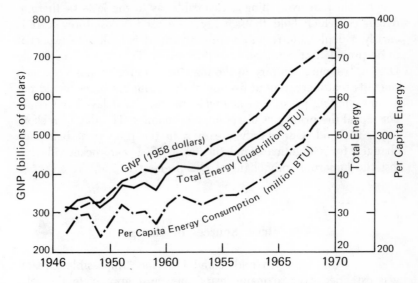

Source: U.S. Department of the Interior, *U.S. Energy Through 2000.*

abundant, cheap energy available to the United States has certainly been an important factor in our economic growth, the sudden change to sharply higher energy prices and limited availability cannot help but retard the growth of the economy and our standard of living.

The Impossible Dream

During much of this twenty-five-year period, the price of several sources of energy remained fixed or decreased. In constant dollar terms, the price of energy fell sharply during most of this quarter century. Energy was a bargain, and we were bargain hunters. As the prices of most other goods and services were increasing, the continuing low prices for energy were an economic bargain and energy use increased.

Energy conforms not so much to laws of Newtonian physics, which hold that everything is reversible, as to the laws of thermodynamics, which hold that energy once used is lost forever. It is clearly a depletable resource and as such, it is foolish to expect it to be provided at constant or falling prices. This is an "Impossible Dream," running contrary to the logic of resource economics which suggests that increasing utilization of depleting resources would not occur at *falling* prices, but at *higher* prices. We delayed but could not repeal the principles of resource economics. The day of reckoning is at hand. Our energy dream is in the process of being exchanged for a nightmare and the twenty-five-year rocket ride has lost the important propellant of cheap energy.

Basic Sources of Energy

To understand how the "Impossible Dream" was extended over so many years, one must appreciate the relationship between the basic sources of energy. Over the last 25 years, fossil fuels (coal, petroleum, and natural gas) contributed approximately 95 percent of the basic source of energy utilized in our economy. Electricity is a secondary source of energy, most of it produced from burning fossil fuels to power electric generators.

The three basic sources of energy—coal, petroleum, and natural gas—are highly substitutable. Since World War II a major shift occurred in the consumption of these fuels (see Figure 6.2). In 1946 coal was the dominant fuel, providing more of our energy than oil and gas combined. By 1970, however, the reverse was true with the energy derived from oil and gas four times greater than that derived from coal. The United States in the postwar period turned to higher quality fuels—easier starting, quickly adjustable, more flexible, and cleaner burning. While the actual energy obtained from coal decreased only slightly over the twenty-five-year period, the energy obtained from petroleum tripled and from natural gas more than quintupled. In 1970, 44 percent of our energy came from petroleum, 33 percent from natural gas, and 19 percent

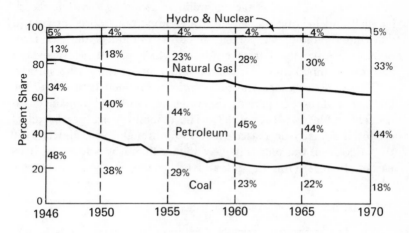

Source: U.S. Department of the Interior, *U.S. Energy Through 2000.*

from coal. Over the same 25 years, the consumption of the secondary fuel, electrical power, increased by more than six times.

The rapid increase in the consumption of petroleum products,
natural gas, and electricity was important in the material advances
following the war. Gasoline, diesel, and jet fuels (petroleum products) were used in increasing quantities by cars, trucks, trailers
and jet aircraft—vehicles of our transportation revolution. Fuel oil
and natural gas were used more and more to heat the growing
number of suburban dwellings. The consumption of electricity
soared in widespread industrial applications and in powering the
proliferating number of home appliances and air conditioners.

Consumers responded to the temptation of low prices for energy
resources and gorged themselves, spending little time reflecting on
their happy circumstances, and when, or if, they would end. But end
they did. Following is an examination of the causes for low energy
prices, the reason for their rise, and why the prognosis is not good.

Petroleum Products

Petroleum products including gasoline, diesel, jet fuel, and heating oils are the most important source of fuel in the United States (44 percent in 1970). Products derived from petroleum are refined from crude oil which has to be discovered and then pumped from pools of oil hidden under the earth's surface.

Even though the demand for petroleum products tripled over the the twenty-five-year period, the price of crude oil remained extremely stable (see Figure 6.3). The domestic price per barrel of crude oil actually decreased from 1957 through 1968, and in 1970 the price of oil was only 3 percent higher than it was fourteen years earlier. In real terms the price of oil decreased about 30 percent

FIGURE 6.3: Basic Petroleum Statistics

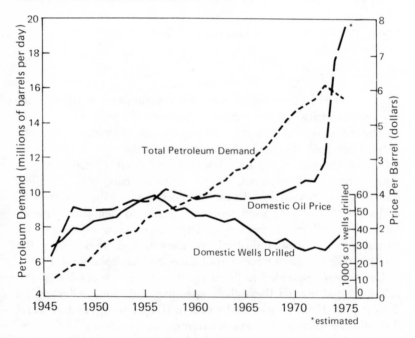

Source: Statistical Reports of the Independent Petroleum Association of America. Used by permission.

from 1957 to 1970. Spanning even a greater number of years from 1948 through 1968, the price of domestic oil increased from $2.60 per barrel to only $2.94, or by 13 percent. Over this same time period, the wholesale price index increased nearly 25 percent. The real price of oil in 1958 dollars actually decreased by 12 percent from 1948 to 1968. When low cost imported oil is added in, the nominal price of oil used in the United States actually decreased over this fourteen-year period and the real price of oil fell even more. Oil was in fact a bargain.

How was it possible for the United States to triple its consumption of petroleum products and, at the same time, maintain such stable prices? It was not because of events in the United States. Fewer large oil fields were being discovered here, the proportion of dry holes was increasing, the cost per foot of drilling was climbing, and proven reserves relative to demand were decreasing. The very price stability of oil argued for less investment in domestic oil exploration. The international oil firms, most of which are headquartered in the United States, increasingly shifted exploration and production to the Middle East, South America, and Africa. Energy self-sufficiency was traded for cheap foreign oil: an examination of this period in more detail will reveal this process at work.

The increase in the price of oil immediately following World War II and the smaller increases in 1953 and 1956 were responsible for a heightened search for oil in the United States. The number of wells drilled increased from 27,000 in 1945 to 58,000 in 1956. Oil reserves increased each year, and more was discovered than used. However, from 1957 to 1970 the domestic price of oil remained substantially unchanged, and the number of wells drilled in 1970 decreased to one half the level of 1956 (see Figure 6.3). Instead of increasing the price enough to keep the United States self-sufficient in oil, low cost foreign oil and petroleum products were imported in increasing quantities.

While the United States was a net exporter of petroleum products in 1946, by 1955 we were importing 10 percent of our requirements, 20 percent by 1965, and nearly 40 percent by 1975 (see Figure 6.4). Foreign oil was so much less expensive to produce that it could be imported into the United States' east coast at a cost lower by a dollar per barrel than domestic oil in 1970.

The "Impossible Dream" was kept alive by substituting lower price foreign oil for increasingly costly domestic oil. Vast discoveries of oil were made following World War II in Middle Eastern countries, including Saudi Arabia, Iraq, Kuwait, Iran, and other countries like Venezuela and Nigeria. These underdeveloped and often one-product economies had limited need for the vast quantities of oil discovered, and hence exported the oil to the industrialized world including the United States, Europe, and Japan. The posted price of oil purchased from these oil producing and exporting economies was extremely stable over the twenty-five-year period, during the first part of which the posted price of oil was $2.17 per barrel and during the second half $1.79 per barrel (see Figure 6.4).

The major oil exporting countries formed the Organization of Petroleum Exporting Countries (called OPEC) in 1960. The OPEC countries were upset over a reduction in the price of oil they were receiving from the major oil companies. Throughout the 1960s

FIGURE 6.4: Growth in Oil Imports and Price of Imported Oil

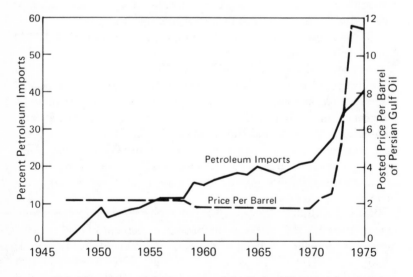

Source: U.S. Department of the Interior and the Federal Energy Administration.

OPEC succeeded in gradually increasing the oil countries' profit per barrel of oil through reductions in the per barrel earnings of the oil companies. The posted price, however, remained constant during this time and was $1.79 per barrel for light Arabian crude oil.

A series of events starting in 1970 brought about a change in the relationship between the OPEC countries and the oil companies. Colonel Qadaffi had overthrown the Libyan government and in 1970 succeeded in forcing the oil companies to increase the price they paid Libya for its oil. This was followed in early 1971 by the Tehran and Tripoli agreements which called for 5 percent annual increases in the price of crude oil plus 2 percent for inflation. Negotiations started in 1972 over how the oil producing countries could eventually buy majority control of the oil producing operations within their borders. The New York Agreement of January 1973 set out a ten year plan by which the oil countries could gradually acquire 51 percent ownership of their national oil.

Over two years (January 1971 to January 1973), the oil producing and exporting countries gained substantial ground in pricing and controlling oil produced in their own countries. However, the ink was hardly dry on these contracts before the oil countries decided the terms of the agreements were unsatisfactory to them. During 1973 the plans involving periodic price increases and gradual takeover were abandoned. The price of oil was quadrupled by the oil countries, and the oil companies' interests were effectively nationalized.

History books will record that 1973 was the year that the underdeveloped oil producing economies asserted themselves. The industrialized economies, dependent on imported oil, had benefited from its constant price and falling real cost. The tables were now turned: the oil-producing economies were in control, and they demanded a several-fold increase in the price at which they sold their energy resource.

Contributing to OPEC's ability to effect such swift and sizeable price increases was the peaking of the United States oil production. Figure 6.5 shows that U.S. oil production actually reached its highest level in 1970. In early 1972 Texas and Louisiana permitted the remaining wells with excess capacity to produce at 100 percent of their potential. The U.S. was producing to peak capacity

FIGURE 6.5: Annual Production of Oil in the U.S.

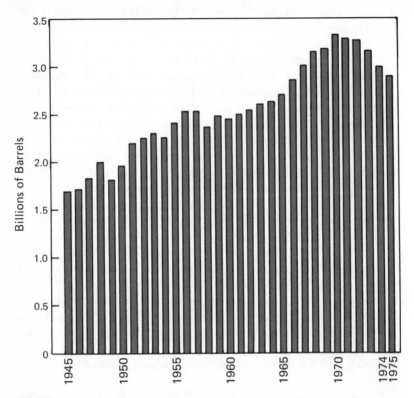

Source: American Petroleum Institute, *Reserves of Crude Oil, Natural Gas Liquids, and Natural Gas in the United States and Canada,* May 1975, p. 24. Used by permission.

with no reserve. In contrast, during the 1967 Arab-Israeli war, the U.S. had been able to step up its output to offset a reduction in the exports of OPEC oil.

Action in the free world now centers around the middle eastern countries of Saudi Arabia, Iran and Iraq, and others including Nigeria and Venezuela. While the industrialized world is experiencing negative, zero, or limited growth, these countries are rapidly expanding. The industrial development plans for these nouveau-riche countries expect growth rates of 10 to 15 percent per year. This expansion is being paid for by the quintupling of the price they charged for their oil from 1970 to 1975 (see Figure 6.4 and Table 6.1).

TABLE 6.1   Price Per Barrel of Light Arabian Crude Oil

August 31, 1970	$ 1.80
February 15, 1971	2.18
June 1, 1971	2.285
January 20, 1972	2.479
January 1, 1973	2.591
April 1, 1973	2.742
August 1, 1973	3.066
October 5, 1973	5.119
January 1, 1974	11.651

The Middle East's gain is largely the industrialized world's loss. Much of the industrialized world's increased productivity must be used to pay for the higher priced oil and thus is not available for consumption by their citizens. Furthermore, crash energy development programs will be absorbing a great deal of the industrial initiative of the developed economies of the world for many years to come. Cheap oil was taken for granted while it lasted. Now we must pay the price of reducing our addiction to low-price imported oil. Energy programs take years to get under way—it could be 1980 or longer before we see substantial progress in reducing our dependence on others for more of our energy needs.

Natural Gas

Natural gas played a more and more important role in the twenty-five years following World War II. At the beginning natural gas resources were largely underdeveloped, but by the end of the period, our reserves were severely depleted. From 1945 to 1970 annual market production of natural gas increased from 4 trillion cubic feet to 22 trillion per year, an increase of almost 450 percent (see Figure 6.6). The importance of gas as a source of energy increased from 13 percent in 1945 to 33 percent in 1970. From 1955 to 1970 natural gas provided close to 50 percent of the growth in energy used in the United States. If imported oil is excluded, natural gas becomes our most important domestic source of energy. In 1973 natural gas and natural gas liquids produced from gas wells contributed 41.1 percent of our domestically produced energy, crude oil 30.6 percent, coal 22.1 percent, and hydro- and nuclear energy 6.2 percent.

There were several reasons for the quickening rate of production of natural gas after World War II. During the 1930s and into the 1940s, much natural gas was simply a by-product created in the

FIGURE 6.6: Production of Natural Gas

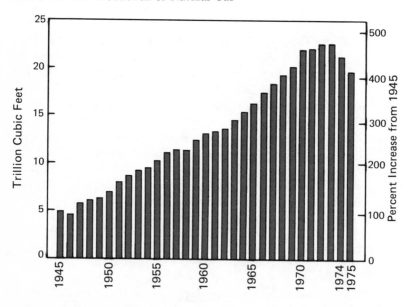

Source: American Petroleum Institute, *Reserves of Crude Oil, Natural Gas in the United States and Canada*, May 1975, p. 120. Used by permission.

search for, and production of, crude oil. The goal of most of the explorations was to find oil; natural gas was more or less the booby prize that was often treated as a nuisance by-product and flared off. But with the discovery of some big natural gas fields in the 1930s and 1940s, collection, distribution, and marketing of natural gas as an energy source in its own right, began.

The growth of natural gas as a primary source of energy is a post-World War II phenomenon. A 17 billion dollar high pressure pipeline system was developed that connected the primary gas producing states of Texas, Louisiana, Oklahoma, and Kansas with all 48 states and created virtually a nationwide market for natural gas, a premium quality fuel. When it became available, it soon competed with coal and oil.

By far the most important factor in explaining the rapid increase in demand for natural gas was its low price, caused by its vast supply—the United States had an estimated 33 years' reserve at the rate of use in 1946. It was a buyer's market, and producers were anxious to sign long-term contracts to gain an insured market for their production. Natural gas suppliers were also fighting for a larger share of the energy market at the expense of traditional fuels, and low price was used as a primary competitive wedge.

By 1960 the years of proven reserves had diminished to 20 years as demand and supply moved into balance. It was at this time that the Federal Power Commission (FPC) started a program of vigorously regulating the price of natural gas sold interstate. The effect of the FPC policy was to perpetuate low prices for natural gas. Traditional rate-setting procedures based upon historical cost and a fair rate of return on investment were instigated. As a result of the action of the FPC, the price of natural gas sold interstate was held below the price of competing fuels which were not regulated. From 1961 through 1967, when the FPC was pursuing a hardline against price increases, the average price of natural gas increased from 15.1 cents per thousand cubic feet to 15.7 cents, or only by four percent. If the period is extended to 1970, the price of natural gas was allowed to increase to only 17.1 cents, or by just 13 percent, during the first ten years of price control by the FPC. By comparison, in the uncontrolled period from 1951 to 1960 the price of natural gas increased from 7.3 cents to 14.0 cents, or by almost 100 percent.

The suppression of increases in the price of natural gas was part of the "Impossible Dream"—the use of increasing quantities of energy at prices not reflecting replacement costs. This ideal but unrealistic situation eventually had to end because the economic effect of underpricing is severe over the long run. Consumption is encouraged and exploration is not adequately rewarded, as happened during the 1960s. Older low-cost reserves of gas were used and depleted, but the price being paid for gas did not encourage the development of replacement reserves. The low regulated price of natural gas stimulated the demand for natural gas but not the supply. Something had to give way and it did. From 1960 through 1967 discoveries exceeded production by only 25 percent, down from the more comfortable level of 75 percent over the prior eight-year period. Since 1968 the production of natural gas has almost

FIGURE 6.7: Discovery of Natural Gas Relative to Production

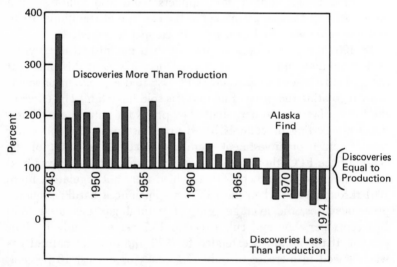

Source: American Petroleum Institute, Reserves of Crude Oil, Natural Gas Liquids, and Natural Gas in the United States and Canada, May 1975, p. 120. Used by permission.

doubled the rate of available discoveries (see Figure 6.7).* Also indicative of our worsening natural gas predicament have been the declining years of reserves in relation to production. Reserves have decreased from a 20-year supply at the beginning of price controls in 1960 to an 11-year supply in 1974 (see Figure 6.8).

The obvious consequence of production exceeding discoveries is eventual shortages of gas to meet market demand. In the winter of 1970 gas companies were forced to significantly curtail the

FIGURE 6.8: Years of Natural Gas Reserves Relative to Production

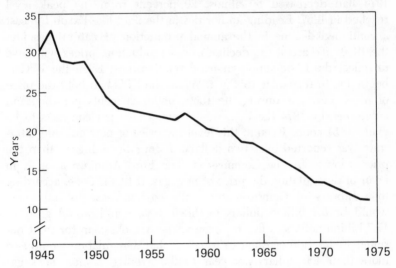

Source: American Petroleum Institute, *Reserves of Crude Oil, Natural Gas Liquids, and Natural Gas in the United States and Canada,* May 1975, p. 120. Used by permission.

---

* A huge natural gas discovery was made in Alaska in 1970, but the pipeline system bringing it to the United States will probably not be completed much before 1980.

sales of natural gas to industrial customers having contingent service contracts. Since then, with domestic production capabilities leveling off, the shortages of natural gas have grown worse. Several gas utilities have been forced to stop accepting new accounts and are faced with rationing supply among existing customers. There were fears that shortages of natural gas during the winter of 1975–1976 might run as high as 25 percent and seriously disrupt business, but, as a result of the warm winter, such a disruption didn't occur.

Production of natural gas peaked in 1972 and 1973 and declined by six percent in 1974. Reported reserves of natural gas at the end of 1974 had decreased by almost 20 percent from the peak level reached in 1967. Leading authorities in the field like Exxon forecast a continued decline in the annual production of natural gas into the 1980s. To arrest the decline in gas production, prices will have to reflect the basic supply-demand relationships. Even the FPC is beginning to recognize this fact. While the FPC had held the price of much new gas during the 1960s under 20 cents per thousand cubic feet, by 1974 the FPC was allowing new gas contracts to be made at 51 cents. Even at this level the price of new gas sold intrastate was reported over two dollars, or four times higher than the price allowed by the Commission. The Ford Administration is in favor of deregulating the price of new gas. If this is done, according to a Library of Congress study, the cost increase to consumers would be 5.4 billion dollars in the first year and would grow to 17.7 billion dollars in five to seven years. A spokesman for the Consumer Federation of America forecasts that deregulation would add more than 400 dollars per year to the average homeowner's gas bill by 1980.

One of the obvious reasons that the price of gas is moving higher is that the United States has already discovered most of the big reserves of low cost natural gas in the lower 48 states. The U.S. is the most thoroughly explored land area in the world, and over two million wells have been drilled in the search for oil and gas. Much of the natural gas yet to be discovered lies in tight structures that are hard to reach and do not contain large reserves. The falling success rate for exploratory drilling and the smaller average size of fields being discovered reflect these difficulties. The best prospects for making substantial discoveries of gas are in the less accessible

FIGURE 6.9: Interstate Price of Natural Gas

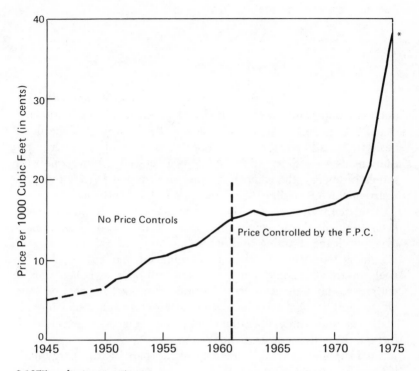

* 1975 preliminary estimate.
Source: American Gas Association. Used by permission.

offshore areas, in the distant and harsh climate of Alaska, and from deep drilling below 15,000 feet. The cost of producing such gas is obviously much more expensive than gas obtained from the major fields already discovered in the lower 48 states.

The energy crisis in the United States would not be so serious if the slackening production capability of one primary fuel could be offset by another. But both oil and gas, which together account for three fourths of our energy requirements, reached peak levels of production in the early 1970s and have since declined. New oil as well as new gas is rapidly increasing in price, a different picture from the small increases in the prices of oil and gas during the last ten years of the rocket ride.

Coal

At the beginning of the rocket ride, coal was our most important source of fuel and provided almost 50 percent of our energy needs. By its end, coal was the least used of the three basic fuels and contributed less than 20 percent of our energy requirements (see Figure 6.2). While coal played a lesser role as a source of energy, the competitive pressure exerted by this fuel was instrumental in holding down the price of other fuels.

After the war, coal often lost out in many of its traditional markets: Residential and commercial space heating was largely taken over by cleaner-burning and easier-handling natural gas and fuel oil; many industries switched to burning oil and gas in place of coal; in the transportation sector the railroads switched almost entirely to diesel locomotives. The primary market for coal was the electric utilities. Yet even here, residual fuel oil made major inroads in the coastal utility operations, and nuclear energy promised to further erode this last great market.

Coal supplies held on to their shrinking share of the energy market to a large extent by maintaining stable prices, or even lowering prices over much of the twenty-five-year period. The competitiveness of coal resulted from mechanization of mining and almost continuous improvement in man-hour productivity. Contributing to the increasing efficiency of labor, was the growing importance of surface mining where huge machines were employed to remove overburden and to scrape out the coal. The competitiveness of coal was also enhanced by lower transportation cost from development of "unit trains" (trains carrying only coal).

The stable price of underground and strip mined coal from 1950 into the latter 1960s can be observed from Figure 6.10.* This favor-

---

* When weight is given to the growing proportion of strip mined coal, the average price of coal decreased over much of the period.

FIGURE 6.10: Average Value Per Ton, F.O.B. Mines, of Bituminous Coal and Lignite Produced in the United States, by Type of Mining

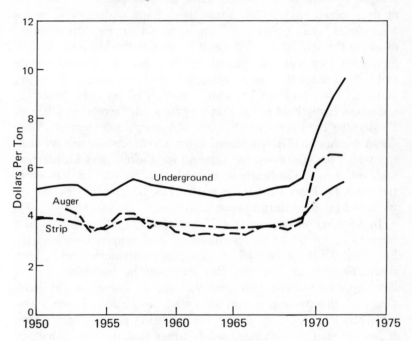

Source: 1972 Reprint, *Minerals Yearbook.* Used by permission.

able coal price situation came to a dramatic halt in 1969. Prices have since been spiraling upward, in many cases double, triple, and even quadruple the cost in 1968. For example, the Tennessee Valley Authority, the largest purchaser of coal, paid around $4.50 a ton from 1948 to 1968, while in early 1975 it paid $20 to $25 a ton. Since then a contract drawn in 1966 at $3.45 per ton was renegotiated at $28.50.

The escalating price of coal has been the result of several forces which almost simultaneously impinged on the coal industry. Changing societal attitudes toward human and natural resources have certainly been an important factor in the price increase. The Coal

Mine Health and Safety Act of 1968 was designed to improve the safety of underground mining. Estimates indicate that the cost of complying with the act added $1.50 to $3.00 per ton to the cost of deep-mined coal. At the same time, many underground mines were closed because they could not, or would not, meet the requirements of the act. To avoid the cost burden of the Mine Safety Act, increasing emphasis was placed on strip mining. However, state and federal regulations were instigated which curtailed strip mining and increasing pressure has also been exerted on strip miners to undertake costly land restoration programs after removing the coal. Finally, the Environmental Protection Agency's enforcement of the Clean Air Act of 1970 has placed sulfur emission standards on utilities which has decreased the demand for Eastern and Midwestern high sulfur coal. The best reserves of low sulfur coal are located in the West, far away from the market. Thus, transportation costs are increased for the utilities.

In addition to environmental developments, other factors also seem to be inhibiting the expansion of coal supply. Utilities have long used the threat of nuclear energy as a bargaining tool to keep down the price of coal—this ploy may now be backfiring. As the coal suppliers became convinced that nuclear energy would dominate coal, they were reluctant to expand production of their seemingly obsolete fuel even in the face of rising prices. Furthermore, it is suggested in Congressional hearings that the oil companies' purchase of six of the fifteen largest coal companies in recent years may be a factor in limiting supply. Their return on investment expectations, based upon oil company standards, could lead to higher prices. Experience has shown that the oil companies know how to limit supply to pave the way for higher prices.

As a consequence of the Arab oil embargo in late 1973 and the shortage and rapid increase in the price of residual oil used by coastal utilities, several utilities have returned to burning coal. Further increasing the demand for coal is Project Independence which calls for stepped up coal production to replace high price imported oil. The Federal Energy Administration (FEA) has required that 41 utilities switch to coal to reduce demand for oil and natural gas. Demand for coal is in its ascendancy and the price is rising even faster than demand.

Estimates indicate that the United States has several hundred years of coal reserves and coal is our most abundant resource. As a result, coal unofficially and officially has been expected to make up for our oil and natural gas shortages. Unfortunately, for the reasons explained, coal has rapidly increased in price along with oil and natural gas and has not provided an effective escape valve to the much higher energy prices of the 1970s.

Electricity

Electricity is a secondary source of energy that is normally obtained from electric generators driven by coal, oil, and natural gas. Sales of electricity have grown by almost 600 percent from 1945 to 1970 (see Figure 6.11), much faster than the 130 percent increase in demand for primary fuels.

The tremendous growth in demand for electricity is a product of our increasing affluence. In the home electricity is the principal source of power for the burgeoning number of appliances. Practically all refrigerators and freezers are powered by electricity. Our principal home-based leisure activities of watching television, or listening to music or radio, use electricity. Also the principal source of power for the luxury of home air conditioning is electricity and businesses have used increasing quantities of electricity per worker to boost output per worker and increase employee morale. The increasing use of electrical equipment in the office such as typewriters, calculators, and dictating machines and the growing number of electric power tools in manufacturing plants and warehouses have reduced manual effort and increased worker production. In order to promote better working conditions, the intensity of lighting has been greatly increased in plants and offices and air conditioning of commercial buildings is widespread, changes that have improved the comfort and employee morale in the business setting.

In the face of rapidly increasing demand, the price of electricity has declined over most of the period from 1945 through 1970. For example, the average price for electricity steadily decreased from

FIGURE 6.11: Energy Sales, Total Electric Utility Industry (including Alaska and Hawaii Since 1960)

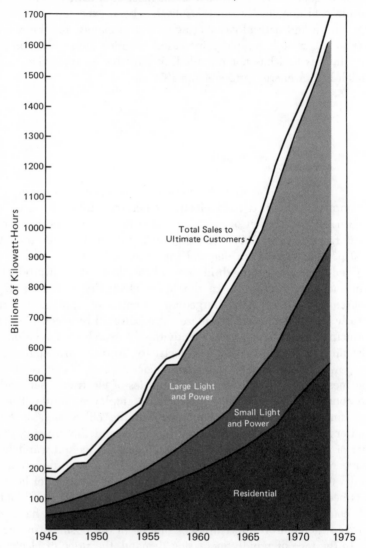

Source: Edison Electric Institute, *Statistical Yearbook of the Utility Industry for 1973*, Section IV, p. 1. Used by permission.

1.86 cents in 1949 to 1.54 cents per kilowatt hour in 1968, and the average price of electricity for residential use fell from 3.41 cents in 1945 to 2.09 cents in 1969. During the same time, the consumer and wholesale price indices have almost doubled. Electricity was truly a bargain. Major reasons for the falling price of electricity have been the stable fuel prices and bigger and more efficient generators that reduced the real capital cost per unit of capacity while simultaneously increasing the efficiency of fuel utilization (see Figure 6.12).

A number of adverse developments, particularly since 1969, sent electricity prices spiraling. As already pointed out, boiler fuels (coal, oil, and natural gas) have increased sharply in price. Since 1969 the average cost of fuel to utilities has more than doubled. At the same time utilities are running into technological limits in generator size and are no longer obtaining large gains in either capital investment or fuel efficiency. The Clean Air Act of 1970 has added to the increasing cost of utility operations by requiring them to make large investment in reducing sulfur and other emissions into the air. Finally, the cost of capital funds has jumped. This is particularly perverse in this highly capital-intensive industry. So the average price of electricity has increased by more than 50 percent since 1969, and in some areas the price of residential electricity has more than doubled. Electricity, the bargain of the twenty-five-year rocket ride, is now much more dearly priced.

Ever since the devastating explosion of the atom bomb in 1945, the prospect of harnessing the power of the atom for peaceful use and in particular for the generation of electricity, has been present. But the history of nuclear generation has been one of continuing delays in meeting forecasted development. Today there are 55 nuclear reactors which generate only seven to eight percent of our electricity. Official estimates that 30 percent of our electricity will be generated by nuclear means by 1980 are far too optimistic. A major problem is that it requires ten years to plan, design, and build a nuclear plant.

The future of nuclear power is still in doubt. Serious questions have been raised about the safety of nuclear plants and our ability to dispose of nuclear wastes. Capacity to produce enriched 235 Uranium may well fall below projected demand by the end of the

FIGURE 6.12: Effect of Fuel Price and Efficiency of Use Upon Cost of Fuel Per Kilowatt-Hour Generated, Total Electric Utility Industry (including Alaska and Hawaii Since 1963)

Sources: 1927-1932, U.S. Census of Central Electric Stations.
1937-1958, Federal Power Commission.
1959-1973, Federal Power Commission and EEI.

Source: Edison Electric Institute, *Statistical Yearbook of the Utility Industry for 1973*, Section VII, p. 1. Used by permission.

century. The main hope for nuclear power in the immediate future is the fast-breeder reactor which creates more fuel than it uses. Unfortunately, construction cost overruns of 300 percent have seriously eroded both the hope and economic viability of this project.

The first full-scale demonstration breeder operation is not expected to be completed until 1982. The jury is still out on nuclear energy, but in the near term this source is not going to provide much relief from energy scarcity and rapidly increasing prices. At best any relief that nuclear energy might provide is still decades away.

Summary

There has been a close correlation between rising GNP and growth in energy utilization. New technologies have been energy-intensive, and large quantities of energy have been substituted for human power in the production of goods and services. Even the consumption of goods by the public has been energy-intensive, and our growing standard of living has been closely tied to using large quantities of fuels.

For most of the twenty-five years, energy prices were quite stable. Taking inflation into account, the real price of energy to the economy was falling, which encouraged still more lavish use of energy. Supply of basic fuels was always ample to meet demand, and there was a considerable amount of competition in the fuel markets. However, as the 1960s became the 1970s, our energy options which had held down prices became badly eroded. In the 1970s all energy prices shot upward to a new plateau that was more than double the level of the 1960s.

The existence of low-price oil imports allowed us to maintain or even reduce the cost of raw materials for our refineries. Events of the early 1970s have demonstrated beyond all doubt that the oil exporting countries have closed this low cost energy valve: The price of imported oil has quintupled. With the continued existence of the effective OPEC cartel, higher prices loom on the horizon.

Similarly, the price of natural gas was artificially held down by the action of the Federal Power Commission. The effect of this policy has been to underwrite the expansion of demand for this premium fuel while simultaneously having a deleterious effect on incentives for exploration. The results were predictable: our reserve stock of natural gas has dwindled, cheap gas has disappeared, and shortages are occurring with frequency.

In the last quarter century, coal was the stepchild of our primary energy sources. Market after market was lost to other fuels. Competitive pressure, significant technological improvements in mining, and the increasing emphasis toward surface mining combined to keep coal prices relatively stable or actually declining. The effects of the Mine Safety Act, limitations on strip mining, sulfur emission standards, and soaring prices of other fuels have resulted in an explosion of coal prices.

Electricity, as our major secondary source of energy, has mirrored the events which have occurred in the fossil fuels—as their cost increased, the cost of generation increased. Technological improvement in generating efficiency, which had been so prevalent in the past, seems to be disappearing today. The result of these two occurrences is reflected in the soaring rates for electricity.

The United States has exited from a twenty-five-year period during which nominal prices were constant and real prices were falling much of the time. Almost overnight energy costs have climbed to double or triple their earlier levels. This change in the price for energy will have serious consequences for the economy and societal well-being for years to come. Already dislocations have been created in industries dependent on low energy prices either for production or their products.

The airlines have been sent reeling from escalating jet-fuel prices, and the passenger market for air travel has stopped growing. The farmer has to contend with sharp increases in both fertilizer and gasoline costs which have been passed on in higher food prices. Homeowners have opened the monthly electric bill in anger and disbelief. Fuel escalator clauses and rate increases have made the air conditioner a real luxury. Even the sacred automobile has been a victim of the energy crunch. A life style dependent on the automobile for basic transportation is already being forced into a painful change by ever increasing gasoline prices. This trend has been most apparent in the type of car being purchased and that being shunned by the American consumer. The autoworker and the motel operator have surely felt the effects of higher energy prices through unemployment. As U.S. households pay more for electricity, more for food, and more for basic transportation, there is less to spend on other consumer goods. As purchasing power is cut, so is employment and production in industries dependent on the discretionary dollar. Paying more for vital energy needs means having less with which to purchase other goods and services.

Most members of society dimly perceive the changes yet to come or even the form these changes are likely to take. The history of the U.S. economy reveals a close relationship between energy use and growth in the national product (GNP). It is safe to say that a decline in energy consumption owing to high prices will initially lead to a decline in the rate of economic growth. Our economy and its life style, built as they were on cheap and abundant energy, are in an untenable position given the new plateau of energy prices.

chapter seven

The Prophets That Failed

The post-World War II quarter century was good not only for most Americans, but also for the discipline of economics. As the American economy continued to grow with only mild and occasional setbacks, the prestige of the economists was elevated. Yet earlier chapters of this book have documented, that the strength of the economy was largely the result of the convergence of three reinforcing sources of economic growth following World War II—large, unexploited, technological opportunity; cheap and abundant energy resources; and a progrowth societal ethic—the three forces largely responsible for the "golden era" in the history of the American economy. Nonetheless, the economics profession was a primary beneficiary of the performance of the U.S. economy. Economists were heard in the highest councils of government, and phrases of economic jargon entered the everyday speech of most Americans.

In retrospect there is a nagging question: How much of this success was the result of the soundness of the theories and policy tools of the economist, and how much was due to the basic strength of the economy? While it is easy to be a successful rainmaker in a tropical rain forest, the real test comes in the desert.

Unfortunately the American economy has recently resembled more a desert than a rain forest. Growth has not only slowed down but in some recent years even turned negative. The models, tools, and techniques are now being tested against a harsher reality. Economic forecasts have been consistent recently—consistently wrong. The world has refused to behave in the manner predicted by their models.

The years of the 1970s are sobering for economists. The persistent fear that their discipline is intellectually unprepared to accept the challenge of the new reality is increasingly voiced—most often by those outside the profession, but also by a few within. Has the profession misinterpreted the twenty-five-year period of prosperity? Has it tried to remake economics in the image of a physical science? In its rush to develop and apply mathematically sophisticated models, has it traded elegance for realism? In an attempt to apply its increasingly complicated statistical techniques, is it guilty of the all-too-human temptation to measure that which is easiest to measure and treat everything else as a constant?

Economics in 1930: Tarnished Elegance

To understand economics in the 1970s, recent economic history must be reviewed briefly. From 1890 to 1930 the elegance of the economist's intellectual approach was impressive—it explained everything; everything fit into place. Economics was a unified science, not the splintered, diverse collection of theories observable today. Marshall's economics was one theory: everything related in a meaningful way to everything else. The theory of economic activity rested on three pillars. First, no general overproduction of goods and services could exist (this is Say's Law); hence there would always be a wage at which everyone who wanted to work could work—involuntary unemployment was impossible. Second, all savings were automatically transformed into real, productive investment. Third, the level of prices was directly related to the rate of growth of the money supply.

The economy was likened to a natural system that was expected to be self-adjusting over a length of time. Participants in the economy were assumed to be rewarded in proportion to their contributions to production, and the system was felt to be morally sound. If one were willing and able to work, a job would exist, and one would always be paid according to the value of one's work. This theory was labeled neoclassical economics. The neoclassical economists, extolling the virtues of free private enterprise, could only conclude by condemning government interference in economic and, by extension, in social affairs. No matter how well-intended, state interference in the private market place could only aggravate economic problems. Contemplating his system, characterized by equity, justice, and freedom from coercion, the neoclassical economist's air of self-satisfaction is understandable—what he said was right, and he knew it.

Like a Utopian dream, neoclassical economics had lost touch with reality and within a period of five years in the 1930s, the sand castles of neoclassical economics collapsed. In England (the bastion of neoclassical orthodoxy) the unemployment rate was above 10 percent from 1920 to 1940, when World War II was well under way. A fundamental postulate of neoclassical economics was that unemployment could only exist if people did not wish to work. Yet the lengthening of the bread and unemployment lines made it increasingly difficult to convince the laid-off workers and the politicians of the truth of this claim. Unemployment in the United States was of chilling severity. For the decade of the 1930s, an average of more than 15 percent of the population was unemployed; and in 1933, 23.5 percent of the labor force was unemployed—almost one out of every four workers (see Figure 7.1). Gross National Product fell sharply, recovering the level reached in 1930 only after the onset of World War II (see Figure 7.2).

An eleven-year depression was not a temporary aberration; yet the economists had been saying from 1929 that the Depression would surely be short-lived. Economist after economist made the trek to Washington and carried the same message: the road to recovery is paved by a balanced budget and noninterference by government in the economy.

Franklin Roosevelt ran his campaign for the presidency in 1932

FIGURE 7.1: National Unemployment Rate

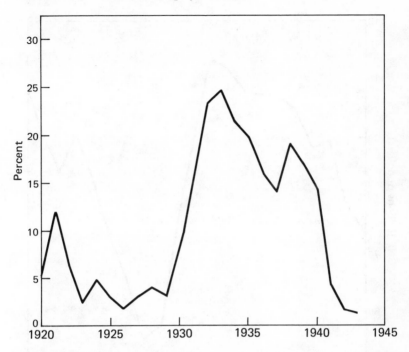

Source: U.S. Department of Commerce, *Long-term Economic Growth: 1860–1965.*

on the old economic orthodoxy: his platform called for a balanced budget and a minimum role for government. Yet, when faced on the one hand with the political and humanitarian realities of the day and on the other hand with the advice of economists, President Roosevelt chose reality. He proposed a hodgepodge of policies and programs, none of which was based on any systematic view of how the economy operates. Instead, they consisted of bits and pieces that had been parts of populist, socialist, and even fascist proposals for a number of years. He made the decision that something beats nothing; anything and everything that had any wild chance of working was tried. Although many of the programs contradicted one another, action was taken during the first hundred

FIGURE 7.2: Gross National Product

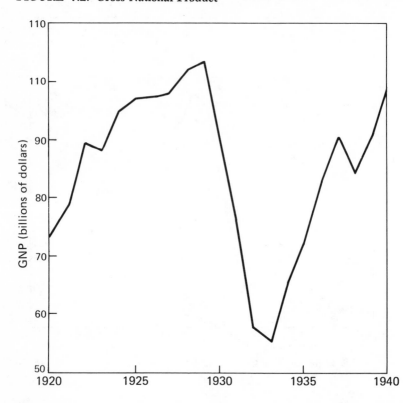

Source: U.S. Department of Commerce, *Long-term Economic Growth: 1860–1965.*

days of the New Deal. The advice of the economists was "observed in the breach," and the role of government changed from spectator to participant in the economy.

Keynes to the Rescue

Events forced the economists to examine the relevance of their theory. This examination was led by John Maynard Keynes, one of England's foremost economists, who had gained his academic credentials by doing superior work that was completely within the tradition of neoclassical economics. Keynes was not only an academic economist, but also a man with considerable experience in business and financial affairs. This dual perspective contributed to his development of a new theory of national economic behavior that was particularly relevant to the problems of the mid-1930s.

Keynes attacked two of the basic principles of the neoclassical system: One was Say's Law and the implied impossibility of prolonged involuntary unemployment; the other was the concept that the interest rate served as the nexus which automatically resulted in all savings being translated into productive investment. In other words, Keynes challenged the basic macroeconomic foundations underlying the neoclassical system.

At the same time, the neoclassical vision received another blow on an altogether different front. The English economist, Joan Robinson, published *The Economics of Imperfect Competition* in 1933 and in the same year, a Harvard economist, Edward Chamberlin, came out with his *Theory of Monopolistic Competition*. Both works demonstrated that we should not expect all markets to behave in a perfectly competitive manner. As a consequence profits and wages may be the result of one's ability to rig markets instead of the traditional reward for efficiency and production. Income payments were no longer seen as necessarily proportional to the contribution to production.

These dual attacks in the 1930s caused neoclassical economics to lose much of its rational unity and moral rightness. Economists who, five years earlier, seemed to possess an answer to virtually all social problems were faced with the distinct possibility of having an answer to none. Additionally, economists along with businessmen, utility executives, and the like, had received an extremely bad press during the 1930s. The profession was in an advanced state of shock.

Keynes not only attacked neoclassical economics, but also presented a new view of how the economy operated. His book entitled *The General Theory of Employment, Interest and Money,* was a remedy for curing the obstinate ills of heavy unemployment and idle capacity. Given the urgency of the situation, the high priest of economic orthodoxy could no longer indulge in self-admiration. Galbraith put it so elegantly: "It is necessary, however unpleasant, to listen to the candid man who had something to say by way of remedy. This listening is the terrible punishment the Gods reserve for fair weather statesmen."

Keynesian economics arose from the Great Depression, providing a set of tools which the economists could use to revive the economy over the *short run*. The major social problem was unemployment, and hence the major social goal was full employment of labor and other resources. Keynes' preoccupation with aggregate demand and short-run antirecession policy led him to deliberately ignore long-run economic issues and problems; so, but less deliberately, did his disciples. Lord Keynes is almost as well known for his quip that "in the long run we're all dead," as he is for his economic theory which contained this short-run focus as its basic premise.

Keynes demonstrated that the short-run equilibrium national income is not likely to be a full-employment equilibrium. The basic goal of the Keynesian system was to indicate how—primarily through governmental spending and tax policy (fiscal policy) and secondarily through governmental control of the money supply (monetary policy)—unemployed workers and capital could be put back to work. The concommitant effects on economic growth were not explored.

Keynes' analysis of the operational characteristics of the economic system was at a high level of aggregation and abstraction. He was concerned with the overall level of supply and demand, placing almost exclusive emphasis on total demand to the relative exclusion of supply. Total (or aggregate) demand includes consumption of goods and services, investment by businessmen, and governmental purchase of goods and services. Keynes' central contention was that total demand was not necessarily sufficient to ensure the full employment of all labor and other resources. It follows that unemployment can be corrected by "pump priming," or as Keynes stated in a letter to *The New York Times* on December 31, 1933: "I lay overwhelming emphasis on the increase in national purchasing power resulting from governmental expenditures financed by loans." In contrast, the unaided employment of resources was a central contention of neoclassical economics under the rubric of Say's Law.

The simplicity of the Keynesian system is its strongest point and at the same time one of its greatest defects—the process of aggregation exchanges complexity for simplicity. Billions of transactions involving, for example, individuals, households, firms, industries, are lumped together under the Keynesian "consumption function." Accordingly, we can now examine effects of all the individual decisions in terms of a single concept. In the process of aggregation, however, we tend to lose appreciation of the diversity, motivation, and complexity found in a modern economic system. Similarly, purchases of plant, equipment, and inventory by large corporations, sole proprietorships, and farmers and the purchases of homes by families are all called private "investment." Much information is lost in the aggregation process.

Using this aggregate analysis, government policy makers can evaluate the economy's performance in several ways. First are the rates of unemployment and inflation. Strictly speaking, pure Keynesian economics would tell us that in an optimally administered (or "finely tuned") economy one can have both full employment and price stability. Over the last twenty-five years it has become increasingly apparent that there is often a trade-off between more employment and less inflation. Neo-Keynesianism has incorporated this concept into the basic framework in the so-called "Phillips Curve." Policy makers attempt to strike a balance between the two evils of inflation and unemployment.

Another indicator of performance is the real Gross National Product (GNP). In the 1960s neo-Keynesians popularized a more useful measure, the GNP "gap." In a given year an economy produces a certain amount of goods and services, the actual GNP. If the economy had used all of its resources, i.e., if no one was unemployed, the economy could have produced a greater amount of goods and services, the "potential GNP." The difference between potential GNP and actual GNP is the GNP gap.

Much of the attractiveness of the Keynesian system was lent by the third component of demand, government spending. Any deficiency in the other two components of total demand, private consumption and private investment, could be offset by simply boosting public expenditures. Moreover, the state could alter taxes to encourage increased expenditures by consumers or to encourage capital expenditures by businessmen. The government's use of its taxing and spending power to affect the level of aggregate demand and, indirectly, employment, is called "fiscal policy." Alternately, the government may encourage increases in total demand through its control over the money supply. By making more money available at presumably lower interest rates, investment activity may increase. In the Keynesian framework, fiscal policy (government purchases and tax policies) is generally felt to be more potent than monetary policy (changes in the money supply) for inducing greater economic activity.

Although the Keynesian doctrine was more partial and restricted than its neoclassical rival, it greatly appealed to economists. It was pragmatic. It gave them an alternative to throwing up their hands helplessly in the presence of large scale unemployment. Keynesian economics provided the opportunity of controlling one's fate rather than being controlled by it. Given the disparate character of the discipline then, any workable theory, even a partial theory and a simplistic one, was better than no theory at all.

In retrospect, Keynesian economics tended to validate some of the New Deal Programs such as the Public Works Administration. But many New Deal programs were advocated and implemented for reasons other than Keynesian doctrines. Federal government budget deficits were often unintended and were relatively modest given the then current economic conditions. Attempts to explicitly use increases in government expenditures to compensate for inadequacies in private consumption and investment expenditures were hesitant at best. With Pearl Harbor all of this changed.

World War II not only gave the Democratic administration and its economists an opportunity to exercise control over the economy, but also tended to validate Keynesian doctrines in an impressive way. Huge deficits were encountered; yet the world did not cave in. Inflation was more or less successfully controlled. The United States defeated the Japanese and the Germans and in the process eliminated unemployment and much of the remaining resistance to Keynesianism. In 1944, even though we were spending about half of our Gross National Product for the war effort, we still managed to produce more civilian goods than we did in 1938. An economy that had had an average unemployment rate of 15 percent for almost 10 years, suddenly enjoyed almost zero unemployment. An economy in which highly trained engineers were jobless, suddenly became an economy in which even their mothers and grandmothers, who had never previously held a job outside the home, were working in factories, producing military or civilian goods. The effect of the ascension of Keynesian economics and our wartime experience was to change economics from a *dismal science* to a *science of hope.*

The second battlefield of the Keynesian revolution took place within the circle of economists (the first having been national politics). The opposing camps were often separated by age as well as point of view. The relevancy of the Keynesian model to the particular conditions of the 1930s, and to the wartime economic problems of the home front, powerfully and intuitively appealed to the young entrants into the profession. The older orthodox neoclassical school fought a losing battle. They were trounced thoroughly, both by attacks on the essentials of their theories and by the bankruptcy of their policy prescriptions. The Keynesian system, with its claim to superior social relevance and intellectual distinction, gained the ascendance. If the economist could no longer be a philosopher, he could at least be an engineer. He could become the technician serving society by ridding it of unwanted effects like unemployment, depression, and the business cycle.

The Emergence of Neo-Keynesianism

The newer breed of economists, consisting of far fewer philosophers than of engineers and technicians, were often not surprisingly based at the Massachusetts Institute of Technology, which became a leading center of Neo-Keynesianism. Unlike Keynes, who was an astute observer of economic events as well as the history of the profession, his disciples gutted the theory of its historical sensibility. Many of the converts to Keynesianism traded in his insightful constructs for overly elaborate sophistications. The gains in realism were minute; the losses in terms of simplicity were enormous. By the mid-1960s, this process was sufficiently complete for economists to wonder aloud whether Keynes was a Keynesian. Many economists seem to agree that the neo-Keynesians had changed Keynesian economics into something unacceptable to Keynes himself. Some old time Keynesians, among them Abba Lerner and Joan Robinson, both of whom fought for the Keynesian revolution on the barricades, have repeatedly raised their voices in angry protest with much courage, though little impact.

The modern economist traded his humanist's robe for the apparatus of the physical scientist. From a single interconnected system that explained everything, economics became increasingly a collection of partial theories that explained bits and pieces—a disparate assortment of subdisciplines. Progress in economics could be made a step at a time by incremental improvements in models and theories.

Economists became amateur mathematicians, learning to express everything in mathematical terms and to use mathematical notations of increasing complexity and elegance. The mathematical trappings gave the profession the semblance of objectivity and of scientific validity not found in the previous, classical conception of economics. At the same time, it did not take economists long to convince themselves that their endeavor, while scientific was also objective, positive, and "value free."

The adoption of mathematics also improved the mystique associated with the profession and strengthened its elitism. Since the nonprofessional could not read what was in an economics journal, how could he attack its validity? Heavy use of complex mathematical constructs based on assumptions more often implicit than explicit kept out the riffraff—merely meeting a payroll did not give one the right to have an opinion about economic issues.

Indicative of the change occurring in the discipline was the training of young economists. In many programs, especially among the leading departments, more time was devoted to teaching higher level calculus, matrix algebra, linear and nonlinear programming, in addition to emphasis on statistics and econometrics, than to more traditionally defined economics. Students took the vows of the "invisible college." Sophisticated mathematics, statistical dexterity, and elegance of theory were paramount. Economists tried to become a new breed of social science technicians, plugging in the numbers and reading out the results.

Economics, like any learned profession, maintains many visible as well as invisible controls upon its members. The changing perception of what economics should be, and of what economists should do, was transmitted through a very elaborate reward and punishment structure. The discipline required that to have status within the ranks, one must be mathematically sophisticated, statistically strong, and theoretically inclined. The use of mathematical symbols and their manipulation to present economic ideas, no matter how trivial, became almost a fetish in the 1950s and 1960s. In order to be published in the best journals, to graduate from the best schools, and to be apprenticed to the best universities as an assistant professor, it was imperative to conform to this new conception of economics as something in the mode of the physical sciences.

The introduction of mathematics into economics has in many cases proven quite useful. It can provide a clarity of expression and a simplicity of exposition difficult to equal with words alone. Unfortunately, there are also dangers of introducing this methodology into what is a social, not a physical, science. The world of the social scientist is not necessarily arithmorphic; that is, the economic world we live in does not necessarily operate in a way that can be easily described mathematically. The simplicity that mathematical expression offers may quickly turn into oversimplification.

A second danger which can be equally destructive is perhaps stated best by economist Marc Roberts: "The lure of formalist virtuosity can seduce us away from the initial focus of our inquiry." A review of articles in prominent economic journals leads us to suspect that they were written not to increase one's understanding of some moderately important economic phenomenon, but instead to dazzle one's colleagues with the brilliance of the author's mathematical abilities. Often no attempt is made to relate the subject matter of the article to any economic problem, real or imagined.

As part of the new image of economics as a physical science, economists claim that theirs is a value-free science. It is doubtful whether even physical sciences can be so described. Thomas Kuhn, in his brilliant book, *The Structures of Scientific Revolutions,* has persuasively argued that even the so-called natural sciences are hopelessly subjective and value-ridden. With respect to a social science his case can be easily strengthened. In anything as complicated as man's economic activities, some conception of the universe must be in the mind of the investigator in order to begin any investigation. Facts cannot organize themselves. In choosing the questions to ask and the methods to use, the investigator imposes his conception of the universe onto his study. Is it surprising that economists, who start with the concepts of economic man and perfect competition, end their journey praising the market system?

Although economists have been better than most social scientists in making their assumptions explicit, the assumptions usually appear in the first paragraph of the work, while the results appear in the last. Economists succumb easily to the all-too-human temptation of forgetting their critical assumptions when they make their policy prescriptions.

Economics indeed does *not* enjoy the simplicity of the physicist's world. There constants like speed of light and the weight of matter are truly constant. By contrast, in studying the economic aspects of man's motivational behavior, "constants" have a way of changing and the whole makeup of the testing ground is in a state of continual flux. The researcher may often find himself working within an interactive environment. The very success of the Keynesian doctrine has, in and of itself, had an effect on the economic relationship on which the system is based. The constants have changed again and are continuing to change. The neo-Keynesians have neither recognized nor understood the change. They therefore see no reason to even consider changing their policy prescriptions.

As Keynes once said, "The ideas of economists and political philosophers, both when they're right and when they're wrong, are more powerful than is commonly understood. Indeed, the world is ruled by little else." Keynes was right when he also said that "Practical men, who believe themselves to be quite exempt from any intellectual influences, are usually the slaves of some defunct economist." The ideas espoused by influential economists change the environment in which economic decisions are made.

Recently, a few prominent economists have had the courage to cry out against the direction being taken by modern economics. Wassily Leontief, a Nobel Laureate economist, commented on the "fundamental imbalance in the present state of our discipline." He continued, "The weak and all too slowly growing empirical foundation clearly cannot support the proliferating superstructure of pure, or should I say, speculative economic theory." E. H. Phillips Brown, in his presidential address to the Royal Economics Society, Britain's leading economics association, stated that "we cannot get more knowledge of causality out of a statistical fit than we put into the behavioral equations that are fitted." Brown argued that economics had chosen poorly when it selected the physical science mode.

The Apparent Victory

The academic Keynesians were victorious on two battlefields: in national politics and within the universities. The Employment Act of 1946 codified their political victory. Although this act was not purely Keynesian, as some of the more committed of the Keynesians would have liked, the federal government was made responsible for maintaining full employment. Just a dozen years earlier economists would have argued almost unanimously that the government was incapable of insuring full employment. In 1946 the earlier heresy became the national policy.

The Employment Act of 1946 set up a mechanism which placed economists close to the seat of power: Provision was made for the Council of Economic Advisors, a body of economists mandated by law to give economic counsel to the President. The role of the economist was institutionalized, especially as it related to macroeconomic policy. This was a large step toward refurbishing the tarnished reputation of the economics profession.

Although the economists felt they were leading the politicians, the politicians have actually led the economists. In response to the politician's need for economic intervention, economists elaborated their kit of national economic policy tools. The temptation to concentrate on short-run economic objectives was overpowering and in pursuit of these objectives the economists were guaranteed ample work, prestige, power, and money.

Government fiscal and monetary policy are the two control mechanisms of the economy, and much of the debate among economists since World War II has been over their relative strengths. The radical Keynesians of the 1940s held that monetary policy was basically useless, able only to hinder recovery from a recession. Fiscal policy, on the other hand, was seen as all-powerful and its advocates placed great faith in the state's ability to reach and maintain full employment through careful manipulation of federal budget deficits and surpluses. In contrast, the Keynesian Revolution never was able to successfully penetrate the real bastions of monetarianism, such as the University of Chicago. There, under the articulate leadership of Henry Simons, the neoclassical gospel of laissez faire continued to be preached. At Chicago, students were taught that monetary policy was all powerful, particularly in determining the rate of inflation or deflation, and that fiscal policy per se could have little beneficial effect on economic activity.

Between 1950 and 1960 a passionate debate raged between the two opposing camps. For most economists the matter was finally resolved with the compromising recognition that both sides had something to offer. The result was a neo-Keynesian-neoclassical synthesis. M.I.T. economist Paul Samuelson played a leading role in developing this new synthesis. Heavy reliance on both discretionary fiscal and monetary policy was taught as the new economic wisdom in a modern economy seeking continued full employment. The concept of "fine tuning" the economy was born. Preoccupation with short-run policy measures was paramount. At the same time the theoreticians busily made further progress on the road to increasing mathematical sophistication and abstraction.

Needed: A Thoughtful Reassessment

Unfortunately, both for scholarship and for society, economists permitted politicians with their short-run interests to define the major developmental thrust of their discipline.

The politicians' concern with short-run optimization leads to sub-optimal results overall. Between 1945 and 1970, the politicians' penchant for, and the economists' emphasis on, short-run policy was at times beneficial and in other instances less useful in maintaining economic stability. The dials of the rocket could be tinkered with without disastrous results, for the rocket's autonomous thrust was overwhelmingly powerful. Disagreements existed within the profession (witness the debate over the relative strengths of fiscal versus monetary policy), producing more heat than light. Fortunately, the economy was strong enough to withstand the short-run tinkering of the economists.

Successful discretionary economic policy was often an accident rather than a planned occurrence (witness the tax cuts of 1948 and 1954 which were scheduled long before the need for them was perceived). The tight money policy of 1953 and the attempt to balance the budget in 1957 were admitted failures of the economic policy makers during the Eisenhower years.

The tax cut of 1964 was loudly hailed as the realization of the neo-Keynesian dream. It represented a deliberate attempt to increase economic growth by increasing aggregate demand. This tax cut was a success and many economists, intoxicated by what had been achieved, called for "fine tuning" of the economy and heralded the end of the business cycle. Again government policy unconsciously took for granted the basic strength of the economy and concentrated on short-run alterations in aggregate demand. Given the healthy, fundamental condition of the economy, short-run policy was of little consequence. Short-run manipulations only induced more or less oscillation in the upward trajectory of the rocket. For two and one-half decades, our economy was healthy, investment opportunities associated with emerging technologies were available, and investment took place.

Investment plays a dual role. In the short run it adds to aggregate demand, since goods and services are needed to produce the capital goods. In the long run, however, the supply side is dominant. Investment increases our capacity to produce, an effect beyond the short-run horizon of the neo-Keynesians, who emphasized the short-run, demand side of investment to the virtual exclusion of supply considerations. When neo-Keynesians did view the supply side of investment, they tried to relate it to the increase in total demand needed to sustain full employment. They did not emphasize that it is investment that is a major determinant of the future level of economic activity. Aggregate supply is not passive: It is a function of deliberate investment decisions. Government policy, in its year-to-year actions, generally ignores the long-run buildup of capital; yet present capital accumulation is a potent indicator of future economic capacity. For short-run, anticyclical purposes, it makes little difference whether increases in consumption, private investment, or government expenditures are used to stimulate the economy. Indeed, a case can be made that personal income-tax reductions and increases in government expenditures are more efficient and certainly speedier in maneuvering the economy back to its full employment growth path than are increases in investment.

By emphasizing the short run, the neo-Keynesian economists have virtually ignored technological change as a source of growth. Theirs is a more comfortable world of static equilibrium. In the short run, technology like capacity, is "given" or fixed. Over time, technology, like productive capacity, is subject to change without notice. The real world *is* dynamic and not static. The great classical economists, from Smith to Ricardo to Marx and Mills, recognized this fluidity of technology and gave it prominence in their analysis.

Modern macroeconomic texts treat technology, productivity, and resource availability as peripheral subjects, if they are considered at all. These factors are, whether explicitly recognized or not, the very foundations of economic growth. Yet, they have been sidestepped in macroeconomic research, in textbooks, and, as we would expect, in policy recommendations. Instead, the economics profession is still busy elaborating and refining its short-run mathematical models of how it expects the economy to function.

Examination of recent economic history and of the policy prescriptions of both Administration and academic economists shows that economics is a captive to the limitations of the Keynesian and monetarist theories. The policy prescriptions, for good times or bad, are either to increase or decrease taxes, increase or decrease government expenditures, increase or decrease the money supply, or all possible combinations of the above. The flipflop of Nixon-Ford economists in the latter half of 1974 is symptomatic of the prevailing confusion. A call for a tax increase in the fall of 1974 was followed by a call for a tax cut six months later.

The gap between the modern economists' vision of the economy and the economic realities of the day is increasingly plain to the lay public and should be perceived even by the professional economists. The Keynesian system, though partial in nature, did shed light on the harsh economic realities of the 1930s. The major problem then was a deficiency of aggregate demand in a society with underutilized resources. Despite the elaborations and extensions of the basic Keynesian model, and the increasing elegance and sophistication in its presentation, the model remains short run.

Keynes was not primarily interested in the problem of long-run economic growth and its engine, the dynamics of technological advance, and neo-Keynesians continued to happily ignore the problem. The bitter fruit is painfully visible and ready to be consumed.

Fundamental changes in the economy have made it difficult to apply the Keynesian tools and achieve the desired results. The recent experience of double-digit inflation and a nearly double-digit unemployment rate makes it difficult to choose the proper mix of Keynesian fiscal and monetary policy to reduce both simultaneously. A choice between 3 percent inflation and 4 percent unemployment level vis-á-vis a 2 percent inflation and a 6 percent joblessness rate appears to be acceptable to most reasonable men. The choice between a 5 percent unemployment rate and a 15 percent inflation rate versus a 15 percent unemployment rate and a 5 percent inflation rate is acceptable only to a desperate or remarkably masochistic society. Moreover, the persistent worsening in unemployment versus inflation trade-off cannot be explained within the Keynesian system.

Economics has enjoyed the luxury of being largely irrelevant since the War. Society cheerfully rewarded the discipline with both honor and pecuniary gain, at least as long as the economy performed well. Economists credited the seemingly lasting boom to their newly gained insights into how the economy could be controlled. The leading practitioners could build their highly mathematical, elaborately theoretical, superrefined theorems as long as the economy performed. Gold-plated econometric models were willingly supported as long as they predicted good times, and the good times materialized. The economist became the prophet of prosperity, and society was more than willing to honor its prophets.

Harsher times are here: The economy has changed. The economist has oversold his insights and policy prescriptions. The economy in 1976 cannot be healed by the remedies of 1936. The future must deal with increasing the national supply of goods and services, as well as maintaining the national demand at near the full employment level. What we need is a return to reality and a reorientation of economics in the same sense that Keynes represented a return to reality in his day. As the first step, a proper diagnosis of the forces underlying the twenty-five-year boom period from the end of World War II to 1970 is necessary. This should be accompanied by an investigation of the effect of changes in these forces on recent economic performance. Yet, the great majority of the profession continues to place its primary emphasis on trying to regain short-run full employment equilibrium. The patina of the old models, so rigorously, elegantly, and proudly erected makes it difficult to break with the past. The profession has a great investment in a glorious, but defunct status quo.

Economics must reform itself, otherwise it will be displaced as a positive force by future events. Society is losing its patience: Expensive games, talismans, and delusions that were tolerated if not applauded in the past are suddenly seen as inexcusable frivolities in periods of prolonged economic crisis. Another scientific revolution looms on the horizon. Rather than wait until it hits, alert economists will do well to prepare for the event and start examining and discussing the alternatives ahead. The more open-minded they are, the less painful will be the transition.

chapter eight

Rx for Managing the New State of the Economy

The twenty-five-year rocket ride of the economy from 1946 through 1970 was a unique period. This unusually long period of a generally rising standard of living and growing industrial output was the result of the convergence of three major forces that gave exceptional thrust to our economy. These three forces that converged at the end of World War II were a pro-growth societal ethic, abundant and cheap energy, and a storehouse of economic innovations. Our major problem today is that these three sources of long-run economic growth have simultaneously dissipated as the 1970s unfolded. In their place are a societal conservation ethic, scarce energy resources, and a dwindling supply of important product innovations. Gone is the cheap energy that was lavishly substituted for human effort and that increased productivity and made life easier. Gone is the permissive societal attitude which allowed industry to treat the air, water, and land as free goods and thus lower the cost of production. Gone is the stream of very significant new product innovations that created millions of new jobs and billions of dollars of new income for the economy.

The economic problems of the 1970s are very different from those of the 1950s and 1960s. Unfortunately, few realize how dramatically our economy has changed over a short span of years. The prevailing attitude of government officials, business and organizational leaders, and even most of the economists is that, in late 1973, the United States entered into just another recession. To the naïve, this represents only a temporary aberration in the trend of a growing G.N.P. and a rising standard of living. Unfortunately, we cannot return to the exuberant days during the twenty-five-year rocket ride of the economy. For government, business, labor, and the public to act as if nothing has changed and that it is "upward and onward" after a period of adjustment will only aggravate and worsen our economic problems.

The best of the options available to the United States is to plan for a slower rate of economic growth than that enjoyed over the period from 1946 through 1970. But achievement of even this modest goal is not going to be an easy undertaking. Since the economy has lost the support of three primary sources of long-run growth, new ways must be discovered to increase the real output of our economy. For far too long we have overrelied on the gross tools of fiscal (government spending and taxation) and monetary (money supply) policies to direct the economy. They are an inadequate response to the challenging opportunities that exist today. New types of government policies and actions are required if the yield of the economy is to increase.

These new policies must be bolstered and reinforced by massive changes in our society—but pointing out the need for change is much easier than implementing those policies that are necessary to effect change. Change, no matter how badly needed, is always resisted. Most people are more comfortable with the familiar and are reluctant to trade it for new ways. But many of the old ways must be discarded if appropriate responses to our economic challenges are to develop. Hopefully logic and rationality will be applied before the economic situation becomes critical. Unusual wisdom and courage is required of our political leaders, organizational spokesmen, and businessmen to overcome economic adversity.

The first recommendation goes to the very heart of an article of post-World-War-II political and economic faith. Its intangibility does not detract from its importance.

RECOMMENDATION ONE

The fires of expectations must be banked and the American dream reformulated. Society has to come to expect less in order to have more.

The United States experienced a rising standard of living over the twenty-five-year rocket ride of the economy following World War II. With the exception of periods of short-lived recessions, the ensuing years were always better than the earlier ones. Families formed after the war attained a standard of living only dreamed of by their parents. A young high school or college graduate entering the labor force at the end of the 1960s expected and attained much more than similar individuals taking jobs twenty years earlier. This experience of increasing affluence became deeply engrained in the present and future outlook of what the economy was capable of producing.

The theme of our growing affluence was often emphasized in speeches by politicians, businessmen, and economists. Our newspapers, magazines, and televisions told us that the United States was not only the wealthiest country in the world, but that it would remain so . . . almost as if by natural right. During the exuberant 1960s, claims were even made that recessions were conquered and that the economy could be steered on a continuously upward course. A combination of the positive reinforcement of experience and ebullient forecasts led to the development of exaggerated expectations. These expectations provided a strong stimulus to demand and played an important and necessary role in our rising standard of living. Only an optimistic America would have gone in debt to build the suburbs, to outfit new homes with many luxurious durable goods, to buy new cars, etc. Optimism, together with the basic strengths of the economy, enabled America to capitalize on the new technology, the cheap energy and the progrowth societal attitude.

When the economy was progressing, there was more for everyone. Highly trained and skilled professionals, the broad white-collar middle class, the semiskilled and highly organized blue-collar workers, and manual laborers all enjoyed rising standards of living. At the same time federal, state, and local governments were able to enlarge their activities and programs, and businesses were able to acquire the funds needed to modernize and expand plant and equipment. Growth allowed each group to acquire more without taking from some other group.

Each segment of society has developed an organization to press its claims and to guard its positions, creating a check and balance system with many constituencies and many spokesmen. Most obvious are the trade unions like the A.F.L.-C.I.O., United Mine Workers, and Teamsters. But professions also have developed influential associations to do their bidding such as the American Medical Association, American Bar Association, and even the American Association of University Professors. The interests of the poor and needy are represented by civil rights organizations and by officials of the expanding welfare programs. The "war on poverty" actually encouraged the development of this constituency. The truckers, airlines, radio and television interests, and the financial community, not only have private organizations dedicated to promoting their causes, but also have various agencies of government guarding their interests under the guise of public regulation. Unregulated industries efficiently promote their own positions through organizations such as the American Petroleum Institute (A.P.I.), the Iron and Steel Institute, the National Association of Food Chains, and many others. Backing up these specialized organizations are more general associations including the Chamber of Commerce, the National Association of Manufacturers, and the National Conference Board.

America became an agglomeration of organized groups, each zealously promoting its own costly programs and plans. As long as the economic pie was growing, as it did over the twenty-five-year rocket ride, the various groups could press their claims and have their expectations reasonably satisfied. The "elasticity" in the system was *economic growth*—there was more for all. A healthy and vigorous economy could cope with the increasing claims of the various groups, and the economic and social strain was manageable.

Today with the sources of long-run economic growth badly eroded, those same expectations "for more" pose a serious threat to the economy. When literally thousands of organizations press their claims for more, this results in excessive demand which our weakened economy cannot satisfy. With the economic pie remaining constant or growing slowly, the excessive claims of one group can only be realized at the expense of another. As a result enormous friction is built up within the system as the divergent segments of society struggle to increase, or even to maintain, their economic position.

The real danger exists that each group, by trying to get more, may actually reduce the ability of the economy to produce the goods and services that each group wants. The bigger the government spending programs, the higher the prices corporations charge, the greater the union demands and the higher the fees of the professionals, the worse off is the economy. These excessive claims feed the flames of inflation which eventually bring about a contraction of output and a slower pace for the economy.

There are few permanent winners from inflation. Remember the complaining contenders for our economic output during the period of ravaging inflation from 1973 into 1975. Organized labor demanded catch-up wage increases and cost of living clauses in new contracts in an effort to maintain their standard of living. Business claimed that inflation was destroying its ability to acquire the capital needed to expand capacity and improve productivity. Business journals had feature articles on the "capital shortage" and some companies ran full page ads in business periodicals, highlighting the supposed capital problem. Similarly, federal, state, and local governments found they could not afford many of their existing programs, much less implement new ones. As long as the economy was expanding, the appetites for more could be reasonably satisfied, but with the pie constant or contracting, these excessive claims were self-injurious. It is impossible to have more than exists and failure to recognize this truism only creates frustration.

One of the adverse effects of inflation is the way it disrupts capital markets and impedes businesses from obtaining funds to expand and modernize their operations. As inflation accelerates, potential investors (savers) charge a large inflation premium in addition to a real rate of return as the price for use of their funds. This drives up the cost to the firm of obtaining outside funds and discourages new investment. Both investors and the companies become hesitant about making long-term debt commitments. On the one hand, if inflation accelerates, the inflation premium charged by investors may be inadequate; on the other, firms are reluctant to pay a healthy inflation premium over a long period of time fearing a later decline in the rate of inflation.

The effect of inflation is still more serious on selling additional stock. During recent inflationary periods, the price-earnings ratios that stocks sell for have fallen sharply. For example, the Dow Jones Industrial Average fell from selling at more than 16 times earnings in 1971 and 1972 to below 8 times earnings late in 1974 and in early 1975. Less prestigious companies than those in the Dow average found their multiples dropping from over 10 to less than 5 during the same period of time and many stocks were selling at less than book value. To sell stock at such unfavorable multiples severely dilutes existing stockholders' positions and makes it almost impossible to sell new stock.

Inflation not only makes it difficult for firms to raise funds from the capital markets, but also to generate funds internally. The two major sources of internal funds are depreciation and retained earnings. The high rate of inflation means that depreciation, which is based on historical costs, is inadequate to cover the replacement costs of worn-out assets. Similarly, the dollars of retained earnings buy less new plant and equipment.

Another serious consequence of inflation is the hammer-like squeeze that it exerts on the middle class. The middle class has been the bedrock of the American economy. It buys most of the homes, cars, and appliances, invests in intermediate and smaller size businesses, provides most of the savings for conventional home loans, and is the major productive force in the economy. Inflation has eroded the purchasing power of the dollar and at the same time has raised the middle class into higher tax brackets. As a consequence the real income of the middle class has been constant and even declining. The troubles of the housing, automobile, and appliance industries were intensified by the double bind on the middle class from inflation and progressive taxation.

Perhaps the most serious consequence of persistent inflation is its adverse impact on the larger society. When the economic foundations of society decay, they no longer support the political and social institutions. The danger of inflation is that the different segments of society (various claimants on the output of the economy) become pitted against one another. Inflation, if unchecked, will set American against American, labor against management, bureaucrats against the people they supposedly serve, black against white, and the young against the old. Each segment of society finds itself striving harder and getting less.

We have no choice but to temper our expectations if our economy is to be reinvigorated. Continuing to maintain the expectations developed during the twenty-five-year rocket ride, will burden our economic system with continuing inflation and reduce it to a level of performance in jobs, output, and standard of living far below its capacity.

The same people that sold the American Dream of the good life—that broadened the mind to realize the possibilities and that catalyzed the expectations—must now help sell the new "American Realism." It is a much less attractive product to sell and runs counter to the natural tendency of politicians, labor leaders, organizational spokesmen, and economists, who have for too long a time justified their existence by promising more and better. Now, hopefully they can promise better quality, but not necessarily more.

The United States must have political statesmanship to help straighten out its economic mess. What we need is some straight-talking, telling-it-like-it-is, political leadership from the highest level of government to grass roots organizational leadership. Perhaps now is the time to take seriously President John Kennedy's famous charge to America to "ask not what your country can do for you; ask what you can do for your country." The only way for individuals or groups to have more, without making someone else, or the economy, worse off, is to produce more. Regardless of the group or person making the claim, to demand more than one's increase in productivity is to play the classic game of "beggar thy neighbor."

The British economy provides a good example of what may happen to the United States if we continue to bumble along, unwilling to face up to the truth. The major sectors of the British economy chose up sides and fought over division of the pie, rather than working to expand it. Trade unions and management were extremely shortsighted and avaricious. Both *wanted* more without *producing* more. Labor has been unwilling to give up constrictive and protectionist work practices, and management has been notorious for its lack of progressiveness. Much of Britain's physical stock—of plant and equipment—is old and obsolete. At the same time that labor and management were at loggerheads, the government bureaucracy expanded at a rapid rate. Everyone was bent on protecting his own bailiwick and in doing so seriously injured the British economy. Britain now shares the dubious distinction along with Italy of being the economic cripples of Europe. Will we heed the warning posed by our transatlantic neighbors?

There is no alternative but to downplay the pursuit of the American Dream of the good life. Individuals must temper their expectations and accept the fact that tomorrow may not be appreciably better than today in a materialistic sense. To struggle today for more than the economy can give worsens the prospects for tomorrow. The young college graduate must accept the likelihood of many years of hard work and denial before arriving at a standard of living comparable to that of his parents. Labor leaders can no longer promise their members increasing wages unless wage increases are matched by productivity gains. Restrictive practices which protect jobs and limit output are a luxury we can no longer afford. Labor, regardless of what color the collar (white, gray, or blue), ranging from the doctor to the janitor, has a vested interest in producing more. Similarly, businesses should not expect higher profits by restricting output and increasing prices. More efficient production and new, attractive products are the true justification for greater profitability. Government cannot continue relentlessly developing new programs that require an increasing proportion of our economic output. Just because the government can put a man on the moon does not mean that the government can or should solve every human problem. Much must be left to the individual and his willingness to help himself.

If we make realistic claims in line with the ability of the economy to produce and consistent with improvements in productivity, then progress can be made toward stabilizing the economy and steering it on a solidly upward direction.

In addition to discouraging excessive expectations, the United States must effectively manage its resources if the economy and the standard of living are to grow. Over the good years a great deal of resistance developed in the economy to the use of our resources in the most efficient manner. There is no better way to increase the yield from the economy than to return the economy to the competitive process.

RECOMMENDATION TWO

The competitive process should be rekindled throughout all segments of the economy. Particular attention should be directed to those areas of the economy which claim for a variety of reasons to be outside the competitive marketplace.

There are few knowledgeable persons who deny the benefits of competition to the economy. Competition provides the important nexus between what is produced and what is demanded. It is competition which insures that what is made, how it operates, and what it sells for meets the needs of varying types of customers at the lowest resource cost to society.

While many individual producers and groups within our economy concur on the virtues of competition, the natural tendency however is to admire it from afar and to wish it on all other areas of the economy except your own. The competitive marketplace has no compassion; it rewards the efficient and innovative, and punishes the outmoded and inefficient. Protective devices to constrain competition have been advanced by all segments of the economy, some being much more successful than others. Labor unions have their work rules, the professionals have their canons of ethics, college professors have their academic standards and tenure system, all of which restrict competition. Business developed sophisticated schemes to reduce competition, such as price leadership and brand image development. In regulated industries, the regulators often protect the interests of the regulated against competition.

The constriction of competition was bad enough when the economy was young and vigorous. With the new posture of the economy resulting from the erosion of the triad of forces supporting economic growth, the inhibitors to competition are much more deadly. For the economy to continue to grow, greater reliance must be placed on competition to better allocate our limited resources and to increase the productivity from a given amount of effort. If we can rekindle competition throughout society, then standards of living can continue to grow; if not, then "stagflation" and the specter of the English experience is the prospect.

It will be hard to bank the flames of expectation, as pointed out in our first recommendation, but it will be even more difficult to reduce the inhibitors to competition. The vested interests in our economy have worked hard to shield themselves from competitive pressures and they can be expected to fight very hard to protect their achievements. The critical link in any effort to rekindle competition is the political process. The executive, legislative, and judicial branches of the federal government do have the power to act on behalf of competition. The problem is a trade-off between "courage of conviction" and succumbing to political pressures which organized groups can bring to bear on those that dare to attack their practices. The American economy needs politicians championing the larger societal interests, rather than yielding to the concerns of the financially and politically powerful. A populist reform of government is needed, a government by and for the people, and for the interest of society at large.

Industrial Sector

Price fixing schemes, some of which are extremely elaborate, are fairly common in manufacturing. Some of the more candid businessmen even admit this. The problem seems to be concentrated in the industries that produce investment goods, such as steel pipes, bathroom pottery, and concrete, but can be found throughout American industry. Every year some unlucky or less sophisticated violators are caught breaking the antitrust laws. Between 1963 and 1972 a total of 918 business firms were convicted in 130 price fixing cases. The courts assessed a total of fines in the neighborhood of 15 million dollars over the same ten-year period. Yet the criminal lawyers of the Justice Department's antitrust division are not threatened by a diminishing caseload, quite the contrary. Obviously, what is needed is not only more efficient prosecution under existing antitrust laws, but strengthening of the statutes themselves.

Manufacturing industries have been increasingly dominated by a relatively small number of giant corporations. The annual survey of the Federal Trade Commission reveals that in manufacturing, the top 200 corporations have increased their control over total assets from 46 percent in 1950 to 60 percent in 1970. Primarily through the process of acquisitions and mergers, large powerful firms have gained a foothold in markets traditionally served by numerous small companies. More and more of our industries are dominated by a handful of large sellers. In oligopolistic markets, price competition has given way to administered pricing with emphasis on nonprice competition—advertising and sales promotion.

The increases in corporate concentration and power brought with them a corresponding change in the structure of the American labor union movement. Led by aggressive labor leaders bent on impressing their followers and peers, exuberant, and often unrealistic, wage demands have been made. Oligopolistic corporations have succumbed to the strong temptation of agreeing to overly generous settlements and to financing these settlements with price increases. Not surprisingly, workers in the oligopolistic industries—for instance, the members of the United Steel Workers and the United Auto Workers—have been gaining an increasingly privileged position among their fellow workers. The end result is higher prices and inflation.

The problem of improving competition in the industrial sector has been of considerable concern to economists and lawyers for many years. For this reason there is no need to elaborate on the specifics of a program for correcting this problem. Emphasis instead will be placed on those sectors of the economy which have received insufficient attention.

Service Industries

There has been a significant shift in the types of jobs and output in the United States since the end of World War II. The production of physical goods, which includes the output of farms, mines, construction, and manufacturing, has decreased in relative importance, while the importance of the service sector has increased. The number of persons employed in the production side of the economy grew from 25.2 million in 1946 to 27 million in 1970, an increase of 7 percent. In contrast, employment in broadly defined service industries increased from 24.5 million in 1946 to 54.5 million in 1970, or by 122 percent. The growth of the service sector of the economy is to a considerable degree the consequence of increasing affluence. As the standard of living increased there was a shift from purchase of goods to a demand for services. Considerably more of both G.N.P. and the family's budget now goes for basic service areas including medicine, education, law, government, finance, travel, and recreation.

The shift in the output mix towards services poses a serious threat to further improvement in our standard of living. In farming, manufacturing, and mining, significant gains in productivity were made over the twenty-five-year period following World War II. This meant that fewer resources were used for a given unit of output which contributed directly to our rising standard of living. However, much of the potential for productivity gains on the product side of the economy has already been realized, and future gains will be more difficult to achieve.

For national productivity to continue to improve, much of the gain must come from the service sector of the economy. Unfortunately the service industries have generally been unresponsive to productivity gains. One explanation offered for the low productivity of services is their highly personalized nature—many are tailor-made for the customers. Another is that the *quality* of a service is more important than its *cost*. While there is certainly some truth in these positions, they do not exhaust the reasons for low service productivity. Other explanations for the limited output of service industries include many constraints against the competitive process. Often these inhibitors to more competition are maintained by strong political and financial interest groups.

The Professions and Professionalism

One of the more important, growing, and costly segments of the service industry is that involving the professions—doctors, lawyers, architects, engineers, C.P.A.s, and the like. Consider, for example, what is occurring in the medical profession, the anchor to the giant and rapidly expanding health service industry. Its rapid growth has made the health service field the third largest industry, trailing only agriculture and construction. Approximately 5 million people are involved in this business today in comparison to 2.5 million in 1960. From 1950 to 1975 overall health spending increased almost 1,000 percent, climbing from 12 billion to 118.5 billion dollars.

As professions now play a much enlarged role in our economy, the ways in which they operate need to be carefully scrutinized. They have insulated themselves from the pressures of the competitive marketplace, as well or better than any other significant segment of our work force. This position has been obtained under the banner of maintaining high standards of ethics and codes of conduct, having the purported purpose of protecting the public interest in providing quality services. The problem is that the means (the standards) and the ends (quality service) are not necessarily complementary. Many of the codes of conduct severely restrict competition; it is questionable whether or not they contribute meaningfully to a higher quality.

Through their codes of conduct or operating procedures the professions limit competition by:

1. Restrictions on supply resulting from the certification process
2. Proscriptions against advertising
3. Proscriptions against price competition
4. Prohibition of new organizational forms and new technologies
5. Strict definition of professional activities
6. No peer or outside review procedures

The total effect of the above is to make competition in the market for professional services almost extinct. It comes as no surprise that eight of the ten highest-paid groups of workers are physicians, dentists, judges, lawyers, teachers of law, teachers of health specialties, optometrists, and veterinarians.

The professions have convinced the public, or at least the legislatures, that the competitive process will not work in their cases. The recipients of their services would supposedly suffer if professionals were forced to compete like those employed in other segments of our economy. Somehow the presumption is made that the public is incapable of making intelligent decisions on its own about the price and quality of professional services.

On Restriction of Supply

A fundamental relationship taught in all elementary economic courses is that if demand remains basically unchanged, the price of the product or service will increase with restrictions on supply. Limitations on supply are normally the result of setting standards which applicants must meet, or from limiting the number of individuals receiving training in the profession. The archetype of supply limitation is the medical profession's use of both of the above techniques. The American Medical Association accredits all our medical schools and sets the examination standards which medical students must pass before being licensed to practice. Supply is so restricted that even according to the AMA estimates, there are three qualified applicants for every one admitted to medical schools. Furthermore, almost one half of our physicians are actually trained in other countries; many of whom were unable to gain admission to U.S. medical schools. What the AMA has done is to employ an old craft union device that dates back to the Middle Ages. While other professions limit supply, none approaches the success of the medical profession.

On Advertising of Professional Services

The medical and legal professions rigidly control the advertising of professional services, one of the reasons being that professionals are above and outside of the market, and thus beyond advertising, a tool of the marketplace. Somehow it is not "professional" to inform the public of one's willingness and capacity to perform a service for a price. Another reason for not advertising is the belief that the individual is fundamentally too ignorant about questions of health and justice to be able to use the information communicated by advertising. However, prohibitions against advertising by the legal and medical profession sell the public short. Customers buy expensive and complex products in the marketplace and are aided in making their decisions by advertising. The market also develops proxies for quality of service in the form of brand names with brand reputation and with brand ratings by outside agencies.

While doctors are at least permitted to list their names in the telephone book by specialty, lawyers were not allowed this privilege until recently. When setting up a practice or changing offices, doctors and lawyers are only permitted to mail gravestone-like announcements with strict limits on what can be printed. With the almost total blackout on advertising, the available sources of information include word-of-mouth, professional referral, or trial-and-error. These information sources are very spotty and unreliable. In many instances professional referrals are made on the basis of social contacts and reciprocal arrangements, rather than on professional competence. Word-of-mouth information is very imprecise and often is not based upon important factors. The use of trial-and-error methods in culling out the incompetent is costly in terms of time, money, and perhaps even to one's health. The prohibition on advertising is of no help to client or patient; it only perpetuates a dependence on the professional.

On proscriptions against price competition

The branding of price competition as "nonprofessional" rests on the fiction that a qualified person could only provide the services at some given price. It is also felt that established prices prevent the unscrupulous from practicing, and taking advantage of the public. In reality, fixed prices permit even the *scrupulous* to take advantage of the public. Yet, in areas like "justice" and "life," the discussion of price is felt to be inappropriate. The result has been the prevalent practice of setting minimum fees by the A.M.A. and A.B.A. for particular types of professional activities. The huge third-party medical payment mechanism of Blue Cross and Blue Shield and government insurance programs are based on established minimum fees, which in many cases are equivalent to the standard price. There is no effort to encourage and reward the more efficient. The fixed price approach is also practiced by architects and real estate brokers who charge a fee of some fixed percentage of the contract or sales price.

If the advertising of prices and services offered is prohibited, then the information that one provides a quality service at a reasonable price is hard to communicate to customers. Hence, the normal process of lowering price to increase volume of business does not work. Prohibition against price advertising greatly limits the possibility for professionals developing lower cost, volume business, with savings passed on to receivers of the service.

On Different Organizational Forms and New Technologies

Given the prevailing one-to-one client-professional relationship, many of the professions have characteristics of the cottage industries prevalent before the industrial revolution. With the assembly line approach of large-scale modern operations, it is possible to achieve economies of scale associated both with the division of labor and with the use of new technologies. This sharply reduces the cost of services and has the potential for improving the general quality level. But the professions in general have fought most new organizational arrangements which would use new technologies and provide new forms of services. Both the medical and legal professions have opposed prepaid services and clinics which would steer the professions toward larger-size organizations.

It is the diversity of organizational types that provides meaningful alternatives which help to make a market competitive. For those people who want the more personal and costly doctor-patient or lawyer-client relationships, this alternative should be available. Those who prefer low cost, streamlined services should also have that option available. If organizational form in the grocery business had been restricted, we would still be buying from the highly personalized, costly, neighborhood grocery store. But despite the lobbying of the small groceries, the chain store idea emerged victorious. Today we have the choice of buying groceries from the very efficient, low-margin supermarket chains, as well as from the traditional service-oriented, neighborhood grocery stores whose prices are much higher.

On What is Professional

The professions have jealously maintained a very tight rein over what activities must be performed by a highly trained professional. They have included in their list of activities many routine functions that are simple enough to be performed by persons with much less training. For example, Dr. Jesse L. Steinfeld, a past Surgeon General of the United States, estimates that doctors spend 50 to 60 percent of their time performing tasks for which they are overtrained.

The preservation of low-level skill activities to be performed by highly trained professionals thwarts the division and specialization of labor and their potential for providing a service at much lower costs. If the doctor and lawyer were to use paramedicals and paralegals to perform routine duties, then they could give their attention where it is most needed and where their training is required. To some extent this does occur, but, because of the lack of price and service advertising, the benefits accrue to the professionals and not to their customers. Somehow it is ethical for a law clerk to research a problem and draw up the document as long as a lawyer signs it and presents it to the client. If there were competition in professional markets, the same quality of the service, or perhaps better, would be offered at a lower price. A high price is paid for the mystique of the sacred doctor- or lawyer-client relationship. An exception to the restrictive nature of this relationship is the income tax field, which for many years was the exclusive domain of lawyers and certified public accountants. But, in recent years, a varied group of paraprofessionals has emerged. General Motors goes to one of the Big Eight accounting firms, while an automobile worker spends ten dollars with H&R Block. When a profession limits the supply of professionals, direct competition is excluded. When the profession closely defines who can do the work, the possibility of substitution of less expensive (paraprofessional) for more expensive (professional) labor is severely limited.

On Peer Level or Outside Review

Professionals boast of the high quality of their service. They have, however, arrogated to themselves the right to judge the quality of service provided to the public. They act more like old-time guilds, protecting themselves from outside criticism, rather than public servants worrying about the quality of their practice. In fact, internal discipline procedures are used more to punish economic competition than to cull out the professional incompetents. One of the canons of the American Bar Association prohibits a lawyer from criticizing the professional competence of another. Similarly, it is extremely difficult to induce one doctor to testify against another, even in obvious cases of malpractice.

Once entry into the profession is secured, no attempt is made to insure that the professional remains capable. A 79-year old doctor, admitted to the profession in the 1920s is still permitted to diagnose and prescribe with no external validation of his continued competence, although it is estimated that medical knowledge doubles every five years. Many doctors are practicing 1950 and 1960 medicine in the 1970s. Stricter standards are applied even to the licensing of drivers. In many states, drivers must present evidence of a minimal level of skill every few years.

Professionals are supposedly providing services where quality is of the utmost importance. Yet the receiver of the service has no objective basis for appraising professional competence. It is entirely possible for a person with a very serious problem and needing the best of professional services to be cared for by a professional with only minimal and obsolete credentials. As the professions do not certify competence beyond original entry into the profession, the individual is forced, practically speaking, to accept what is available. Doctors who enjoy the benefits of professional courtesy (free service from another professional) are extremely selective in whom they choose to treat their families. Unfortunately the layman is not in the know, and often makes the wrong choice.

What would happen if politicians were the only judges of their own competence? The incumbents would always be found to be the best qualified. This is, incredibly, exactly what we have allowed the professions to do with their self-regulation, and the result is the same. Once a candidate has been admitted to the profession, his continued good status is assured unless "a heinous act of moral turpitude" is committed.

Regulated Industries

Many of the same techniques employed by the professions to stifle competition are also used by regulated service industries such as transportation, communication, and financial services. The constraints on competition in such industries are largely the result of legislation and rulings by the controlling government agencies. Restrictions on competition are familiar: barriers to competitive entry, limits on price competition, and resistance to new forms of services and new technologies. The problem of these industries is that they have been placed in regulatory strait-jackets.

A primary reason for government regulation of selected industries is the protection of the public interest. Unfortunately, in many instances the consequence of regulation is to the public detriment, for several reasons. One reason is that the regulatory process frequently outlives its usefulness. In many instances companies were originally granted monopolistic positions in order to take advantage of economies of scale possible in particular industries. The government then regulated prices and profits to insure that they were reasonable. However, when the need for regulation ceased, the institutionalized regulatory process lived on. The regulated became accustomed to, and comfortable with, the greater certainties of a controlled environment, while the regulators enjoyed the comforts of secure positions. Another problem with regulation is that it spawns *more* regulation. In attempting to solve one problem through regulation, several more problems are often created which in turn require further regulation. The end result is an industry bogged down in red tape. A further difficulty with regulation is the assimilation by the regulated of the regulators. Daily faced with the particular problems of "their" industry, the regulators too often identify themselves with the industries' problems. They often lose sight of their true function, the promotion of the public interest. Regulators become defenders of the status quo and the existing industry practice and structure.

The transportation industry provides a nearly perfect lesson in the dangers of regulation. The public pays an exorbitant upkeep for the common-law marriage of transportation firms and their regulators. The potential for gain is large if the economy can rid itself of the entrenched regulatory process and allow the efficiency of the competitive market to work out its cold logic which grants no favors.

The Interstate Commerce Commission (I.C.C.)

The earliest regulated industry was the railroad, which came under the control of the Interstate Commerce Commission (I.C.C.) in 1887. The logic for regulating the rates charged by railroads was their original quasimonopolistic position. For many markets and many products the only reasonable way to ship was by rail, and the service was often provided by only one or two carriers. There was not enough natural competition to insure a fair rate.

Increased competition in the early 1930s from the emerging trucking and barge industries diminished the railroads' monopoly position. Instead of deregulating the railroads, regulation was extended, first to include motor carriers and later to include certain types of water carriers which were increasingly competing with the railroads. With the rapid development of the trucking industry following World War II, and particularly with the construction of the Interstate Highway System, the monopolistic position of the railroad was further diminished and in most cases ceased to exist.

The I.C.C. attempts to divide total shipping between the alternative methods of transportation, a process better performed by competition than by administration. The status-quo conservatism of regulation biases it against entrepreneurial behavior in general and new technology in particular. For example, in the Big John case, the Southern Railroad proposed a 40 percent rate reduction for hauling grain in large-capacity aluminum cars. It took four years and millions of dollars in legal expenses before Southern was permitted to use a more efficient process and to pass along the benefits to customers. There are many other instances where the I.C.C. does not permit freight to move by the least costly method.

No natural barriers to competitive entry exist in the trucking business. Nonetheless, the I.C.C. maintains rigid controls over entry and over the markets that entrants are permitted to serve, by granting or refusing to give certification of public convenience and necessity to prospective truckers. Not surprisingly, new entrants into the interstate common carrier trucking business have been almost nonexistent.

There are two types of licensed trucking firms: common carriers and private carriers. Only the common carriers are permitted to carry freight for others; the private carriers are restricted to moving just their own freight. A private shipper carrying freight away from a company's plant cannot haul someone else's product on the return trip. The private haulers frequently deadhead back (i.e., return empty) to their original destination because of this regulation. Prohibiting private haulers from carrying someone else's freight on the return trip means higher shipping costs for the economy, more trucks and more congestion, and considerable energy waste.

The total cost of all I.C.C. regulation of the transportation industry to the economy has been estimated to be as high as 10 billion dollars per year.

The Civil Aeronautics Board (C.A.B.)

From its inception in 1938 the Civil Aeronautics Board (C.A.B.) has been charged with regulating the economic aspects of the airline industry. Since 1938 no new trunk line carrier has been certified, although air traffic has increased 500 times. The C.A.B. focuses on making route awards to existing carriers and establishing fares.

One of the few competitive variables left to the airline industry is frequency of schedule. To increase frequency of flights, the airlines glutted the hangars with new planes that were subsequently used at a relatively low level of capacity. In the latter 1940s and early 1950s the airlines filled 60 percent of their seats; by the early 1970s capacity utilization dropped to 50 percent. To compensate for the low rates of capacity utilization, the airline companies requested higher fares from the C.A.B.; these higher fares in turn reduced the market for air travel. The other competitive variables available to the airlines are best described as costly frills—for example, free meals and snacks, free champagne flights, specially tailored hostess outfits, new interiors, special and wide seating, and even free movies and piano bars on long distance flights.

C.A.B. regulations directly and indirectly constrain one of the most effective competitive variables—price competition. In California and Texas where the C.A.B. has no authority, intrastate airlines flourish. They charge fares that are often 30 to 35 percent lower than those of the major airlines for flying similar distances. Recently, World Airlines (a major air charter service company) proposed to fly a no-frills service from Oakland, California, to Newark, New Jersey, charging $89 for a one-way ticket. In contrast, the regulated airlines charge $182 for a coach ticket to fly from San Francisco to New York City. World's proposal was strenuously opposed by other East-West carriers and has been rejected by the C.A.B.

When the jumbo jets (the Boeing 747, DC 10, and L 1011) were introduced in the latter 1960s and early 1970s, the day of mass air travel presumably had arrived. With more than twice the capacity of earlier vintage jets and lower operating costs per seat-mile, the economies of scale of the jumbos appeared quite favorable. However, these economies have not been realized by the airlines or the public, since the jumbos have operated well below their most efficient load factor. C.A.B. restrictions on pricing, new service forms, and new competition have contributed to the disappointing results from the jumbo jets. The total cost in terms of waste and inefficiency resulting from the C.A.B. regulation of airlines probably exceeds a billion dollars a year.

Specific Ways to Introduce Competition

The second recommendation is as radical as it is simple. Competition must be revitalized in the industrial sector and must be introduced into the service sectors of the economy. For too long it has uncritically been accepted that competition is inappropriate in the professions and regulated service industries. The banners of professional standards, ethics, and regulation in the public interest, camouflage massive institutional arrangements for limiting price competition, for thwarting entry of new rivals, and for slowing the adoption of new forms of service delivery and new technologies.

The professions' and regulated industries' defenses against the competitive process and practices are very strong. Previous attempts to introduce competition into these areas have been repelled. The political power of organizations like the American Medical Association (A.M.A.) and the American Bar Association (A.B.A.) should not be underestimated. Obtaining professional reform through Congress, when 70 percent of its members are lawyers, is a formidable undertaking. Business, unions, and regulators coalesce in the regulated industries, preaching a joint sermon on the evils of change. Even the mention of eliminating restrictions on private trucking companies, so that wasteful deadheading can be reduced, was strongly opposed by all the vested interests. The Teamsters were livid about such a proposal, for it would mean fewer jobs for their union members, and the common carrier truck lines facing the prospects of increased competition were equally antagonistic. Airlines are strongly opposed to deregulation, with some companies predicting disaster for the industry. Clearly, with decontrol the weaker companies would be forced to merge and new competitors would enter the industry. Lazy or inept firms would suffer in the marketplace, as they should. The marketplace has no sympathy for the inefficient; the regulators do.

Specific steps for introducing competition into the professions are outlined below. The authors feel that the adoption of these recommendations will bring about greater efficiency and lower prices for professional services. They should also lead to more intelligent decision-making by consumers about the quality and form of service they wish to obtain from professionals.

1. Prohibitions against advertising should be eliminated, and professionals permitted to inform the public about the availability, quality, and price of their services.
2. Professionals should not be permitted to define for themselves those jobs which only they may perform.
3. Professions should not be permitted to use accreditation procedures to restrict the supply of qualified practitioners. The burden of proof should be on the profession to show that accreditation does not have that result.
4. Those professions where quality of service is very important, as in the case of medicine and law, should be issued licenses which must be renewed every few years. The professional would be retested and required to display a satisfactory level of competence before having his license renewed.
5. Professionals would be encouraged to display their test scores according to their quartile ranking (first, second, third, or fourth quartile). Obviously those with high scores would be anxious to display their credentials while those scoring poorly would not be so inclined. This would introduce a measure of quality competition to patients and clients.
6. Eliminate all prohibitions and restrictions on new forms of service delivery. This would increase the number of service options available to customers and result in lower cost services being made available to many.

Greater efficiency and lower prices can be realized in the regulated service industries if the barriers to competition are torn down. The presumption should always be that, unless proven otherwise by empirical evidence, competition is in the best interest of the public. The burden of proof must be shifted to the regulators and the regulated, in order to prove that continued regulation is in the public interest. If a certain aspect of an industry, for example airline safety, is found to require regulation, then regulation should be limited to only that activity and not be allowed to creep into the economic side of the operation. Short of strong evidence that it would not be in the public interest, regulators should be prohibited from controlling competitive entry and prices. Proposals for phased de-control should be cautiously examined, since the time to accomplish decontrol can be so long with the change introduced so gradual, that it discourages new forms of service competition and the entry of new competitors.

The problems associated with public regulation and protection of particular industries are similarly encountered in new govern-ment initiatives in protecting and regulating the environment, the workplace and the marketplace.

RECOMMENDATION THREE

The many new societal laws must be reexamined on a cost-benefit basis. The laws should be revised as needed to insure that society is receiving good value for the massive commitment in resources being made.

The decade of the 1960s, the last ten years of the twenty-five-year period of economic exuberance, was a time during which the social consciousness of the United States was piqued. As the stan-dard of living shot forward with new vigor during the 1960s, in-creasing concern was expressed about the nature of the industrial process and hidden costs of economic growth. The pampered citi-zens of affluence commenced to question many long-standing business practices. When critically examined, the business sys-tem was found to have its imperfections. During this period of self-examination, the negative consequences of economic growth were highlighted and emphasized. Time and again it was shown that the industrial process was a major contributor to air, water, and land pollution; that the workplace and its products could injure and kill both worker and consumer; and that consumers often made decisions in the marketplace with less than adequate and accurate information. This introspection led to an outpouring of laws in the latter 1960s and early 1970s which were intended to correct these newly perceived wrongs associated with the business process.

Unquestionably there was need for improving the way in which business operated. But like so many newly publicized problems, zeal and overreaction contended all too successfully with more reasoned responses. This in part resulted from the fact that it is often much easier to identify problems than to prescribe solutions. Pleas for patience, more study, and greater consideration have too often been delaying tactics on the part of opponents, or have been seen as such by proponents of new legislation. Badly constructed and poorly considered legislation was often preferred on the grounds of taking action, rather than doing nothing. Much of the debate was conducted on a very emotional level and new legislation was set more often with a view of punishing sinners than from the viewpoint of utilizing society's scarce resources in the most socially satisfactory way. Also, tight time tables have been established for meeting new standards even when the technology for meeting the standards either does not exist or else is extremely costly to employ. In addition to difficulties inherent in responding to newly perceived societal problems with appropriate legislation, it must be recognized that societal laws may run contrary to other goals such as energy conservation, full employment and lowering inflation. Some bold initiatives for the United States have been established by the recent wave of societal legislation and before we go any further, we must examine the consequences of these legislative initiatives.

It was in the euphoria of the booming 1960s that the recent wave of societal laws was initiated. When economic conditions are strong as they were during that period, attention is focused on higher order societal issues. During such halcyon times public attention can be diverted from production and consumption activities toward correcting imperfections. However, what must not be overlooked is the impact of the new legislation on business, and in turn on the performance of the economy. The movement towards risk-free living, a clean and beautiful environment and perfect consumer-market information exacts a heavy cost from the economy. A large price tag is tied to meeting the goals of social legislation. Certainly almost everyone would like to achieve the noble objectives written into law, but the so often unasked and unanswered question is *what is it going to cost and what benefits will society receive.*

The legislative history of the societal laws is revealing. Many of the laws were passed during the Vietnam War when the federal budget was strained. These laws had little direct cost to the federal government and support for the high minded laws sounded good to the voters back home. It was hard to be opposed to cleaner air and water, a safer work place, and better consumer information. While these laws were cheap for the government to pass they have been enormously expensive for business to implement. Much of the cost is only being felt after a lag of several years. Standards passed in the late 1960s and early 1970s when the economy was sound are having effect in the middle and late 1970s when the economy is less well. Estimates on the investment necessary to meet the requirements of the new societal laws run from 500 billion dollars to more than one trillion dollars over the period from the early 1970s to the mid-1980s. In addition, the cumulative effect of these laws has been to increase the direct cost per unit of output by business. What all of this means is that huge quantities of scarce resources—capital, labor, and raw materials—are being diverted to meet the changes mandated by the wave of societal laws of the 1960s and 1970s. What is needed before we plunge further into the costly process of meeting the mandates of these laws is a measuring of the benefits to society in comparison to the costs. What is at issue is not the need for these societal laws but rather the reasonableness of the standards set, fairness in enforcement, prescribed procedures for meeting the standards, time allowed for compliance and compatibility of environmental objectives with other goals.

Thus far, there has been far too much of an adversary relationship between business and government in response to the new societal issues. Instead of business charging that government is out to destroy the free enterprise system and government counter-claiming that businessmen are villains, we need and must have a cooperative relationship where practical solutions to problems can be developed.

The steel industry provides some examples of issues that must be addressed in arriving at reasonable decisions concerning pollution. Steel making is a dirty business and has been a significant contributor to air and water pollution in major steel making areas. The steel industry claims to be able to capture more than 90 percent of its fumes by the construction of hoods and exhaust systems over its furnaces. Similarly, the steel industry indicates that it will generally be able to meet the interim water standards set for 1977 which will eliminate around 90 percent of its industrial discharges into waterways. To this point industry spokesmen and many neutral observers alike argue that a rough balance exists between the cost of cleaning up and societal benefits. What now needs to be carefully examined in steel, as well as in other industries, is the cost in comparison to the benefits of removing the remaining pollution. Removing the last 5 or 10 percent of the pollution may be more costly than the entire first 90 percent. In such instances the massive resources necessary should not be committed unless the benefits are commensurate with the cost. The costs must be considered before the resource commitment is made to meet the stringent environmental standards of the 1980s.

Inconsistent policies are followed in enforcing the strict limits and time tables for meeting air and water quality standards. Many of the municipalities are years behind in satisfying the interim standards, while industry is being required to make whatever expenditures that are necessary to stay on track to meet the 1980 objectives. Industry is also confronted with a "Catch-22" type situation in terms of capacity expansion. The steel companies are not permitted to expand capacity where ambient air does not meet federal goals. This situation exists in most heavily industrialized areas. However, even in relatively pollution-free areas where the effect would be to lessen environmental quality, these companies find it almost impossible to secure licenses to expand capacity. This type of situation stymies expansion and could lead to the capacity shortage type of inflation experienced during 1973–1974. Finally, meeting pollution standards in the steel and other heavy industries is an energy intensive process which accelerates as the more stringent standards are imposed. There is some evidence that suggests that the environmental deterioration which accompanies this energy consumption used for pollution control may equal or surpass that which is eliminated in the first instance. All that is then accomplished is site transfer of the pollution at a large cost to industry.

Without clearly recognizing what has occurred, the new societal laws have been given priority over other important goals. The conflict between energy conservation and independence with a pollution-free environment is obvious. Harder to document, but nonetheless real, are the conflicts between the societal laws and the desire for innovation, full employment, greater investment, lower inflation, etc.

The new societal concerns must be matched with proper concern for our growing dependency on foreign oil.

RECOMMENDATION FOUR

The United States should take the initiative in making the world market for oil more competitive.

The free world economies have been shattered by the rapid escalation in the cost of energy led by the increase in oil prices. In many developed and underdeveloped countries alike, inflation has been rampant, industrial output has declined, unemployment has been high, and political and social instability have increased. The long-run consequence of the rapid increase in energy prices could well be disastrous to world economic order and even touch off another war. The stakes are great and decisive action is required before it is too late.

The free world, and particularly the United States, stood by, paralyzed, as the oil producing and exporting countries (abbreviated O.P.E.C.) doubled and doubled again the price of their oil during the final quarter of 1973. Since then O.P.E.C. has tacked on several smaller price increases which have resulted in the price of Middle Eastern oil rising from $2.10 per barrel on October 1, 1973 to $11.29 per barrel on October 1, 1975. With this 400 percent escalation in the price of O.P.E.C. oil, the price of non-O.P.E.C. oil and other sources of energy has soared. The O.P.E.C. nations repudiated agreements with the oil companies which scheduled gradual price increases over a number of years. Similar agreements for the gradual transferral of ownership in the oil company concessions and operations to the O.P.E.C. nations were voided. They demanded an immediate 50 percent ownership and followed that up with total nationalization.

There were several reasons for the sudden turn of events. During the 1960s and early 1970s, the price of O.P.E.C. oil did not increase as fast as inflation. Imported oil was a real bargain and demand for oil grew. With demand approaching the level of O.P.E.C. supply and with the dwindling production of oil in the U.S., the stage was set for O.P.E.C.'s actions. In addition, resentment had developed, stemming from a nationalistic spirit. The O.P.E.C. nations disliked outsiders owning and controlling oil operations within their countries.

Uncertainty and inaction on the part of the United States, the leading industrial power and the largest importer of oil, must in part be held responsible for what has occurred. At the time of the rapid increases during the final quarter of 1973, the attention of government was on other matters and the country had little stomach for confrontation. The President and Congress were absorbed in impeachment proceedings and the memory of the unpleasant military involvement in Vietnam was still strong. When the United States and the other countries accepted the first increase with little flinching, the stage was set for increase after increase until the price of oil quintupled over a two-year period.

Increases in the price of oil and changes in ownership were certainly in order; the problem was the speed and magnitude of these changes and how they were carried out. O.P.E.C. demanded retribution for the low price they had received for oil and the antagonism resulting from outsiders' ownership and control of their natural resources.

The U.S. shirked its duty to protect the economy from the economic blackmail of the oil cartel. Confusion reigned. There were comments that the exorbitant prices could not hold, but after two years the facts refute this position. Secretary of State Henry Kissinger even talked at one time of establishing a floor below which imported oil could not drop to encourage development of domestic sources of energy. On the other hand, Secretary of Treasury Simon tried to talk the price of oil down. Some called for conservation measures and reduction of demand to bring down the price. Others suggested that a coalition of importing countries was needed to confront O.P.E.C. President Ford even pointed out that the high price of oil could lead to war. It is apparent that the price of oil is not going to come down as a result of wishful thinking, rational argument, conservation efforts, voluntary responses of exporting nations, a coalition of importing countries, or even an idle threat of war. Instead, decisive action is required of the United States to break the O.P.E.C. cartel and to bring down the price of oil.

The United States and other countries have delegated the responsibility for maintaining the supply of low cost, imported oil to the Seven Sisters (Exxon, Texaco, Mobil, Socal, Gulf, Shell and British Petroleum). For four decades this arrangement worked satisfactorily. Then almost overnight the Seven Sisters lost their ability to hold prices down and to insure supply. With more than half of their profit coming from the O.P.E.C. nations, and with 80 percent of the free world oil reserves controlled by O.P.E.C., the Seven Sisters caved in and met the extreme demands made by O.P.E.C.

The Foreign Affairs Committee chaired by Senator Church concluded after extensive hearings in its summary report that:

> The primary concern of the established major oil companies is to maintain their world market shares and their favored position of receiving oil from O.P.E.C. nations at costs slightly lower than other companies. To maintain this favored status, the international companies help prorate the production cutbacks among O.P.E.C. members.

While the Seven Sisters have lost their ownership position and control over price, they still perform an important function for the O.P.E.C. nations for which they are compensated. These oil companies conduct the rationing system employed by O.P.E.C. They insure that there are no oil surpluses that might drive down the price to a competitive market level.

It is possible to scorn the Seven Sisters for "going native." But, put in a similar situation, most profit-seeking businesses having a board of directors and stockholders would have eventually given in to O.P.E.C.'s demands. To stand up against the O.P.E.C. cartel a given company stood to lose all; through reluctant acquiescence, however, its position, though weakened, could be maintained.

To hold the major oil companies blameless in what has happened is not appropriate, but the primary fault must be put at the doorstep of the federal government. When the chips were down and the extreme demands were made by O.P.E.C. the federal government was not there to back up the oil companies. President Nixon, instead of attending to affairs of state was trying to cover up Watergate and to avoid impeachment. Politicians of both parties called for the oil companies to show more courage than they themselves demonstrated. Without the support of the federal government, the oil companies could not take a hard stand against O.P.E.C.'s demands and, as a consequence, a working alliance was formed between the Seven Sisters and O.P.E.C.

To date the Seven Sisters have had little choice but to go along with the O.P.E.C. cartel. The cartel is bigger than the companies and is held together by a handful of powerful countries. The cartel must be offset by like power; the U.S. must take the initiative in strongly encouraging more reasonable pricing of oil. The U.S.'s legal position with the O.P.E.C. nations is fairly strong—these countries expropriated properties of U.S. corporations and voided contracts regarding the price of oil. Furthermore, the O.P.E.C. nations have entered into a cartel to destroy the market process by limiting production so that they can charge a monopoly price for their oil.

The United States has considerable power, short of military force, to react to the extortionate level to which the price of O.P.E.C. oil has been raised. We are the largest importer of oil and petroleum products in the world. Six-and-a-half million barrels of petroleum imports per day flow into this country, equal to approximately 25 percent of O.P.E.C. production. This huge market for oil amounts to 25 billion dollars in annual expenditure by the United States. Oil is valuable, but so is our volume market for oil. What we can and must do is introduce some competition for that market. Why should any country like Venezuela have a guaranteed access to the U.S. market? That is something to be earned and deserved, and with the cartel and the quintupling of prices, no one is deserving of a guaranteed market. If Venezuela or any other country wants guaranteed access to U.S. business, it must earn this right.

The U.S. must insist on competitive pricing of the oil it purchases. The U.S. should announce that it is prepared to receive bids for varying quantities of oil which it imports. Contracts would be awarded based upon the price and terms offered by the different oil exporting countries. To date there has been no incentive for countries to break from the cartel and it is up to the U.S. to provide these incentives. Furthermore, the U.S. also should notify the cartel that it will not tolerate another economic boycott as occurred in October 1973. That was an act of war but then the United States was too weak to respond. Today it is a different matter and the United States should let O.P.E.C. know it means business. In the past the United States has acted hesitantly in dealing with the O.P.E.C. cartel; it must now act as a mighty industrial and military power.

The fundamental changes that have occurred in the state of the American economy require that the economics profession reorient itself. A major shift in emphasis must occur if the profession is going to make a meaningful contribution to properly managing our economy.

RECOMMENDATION FIVE

Economists must become relevant and recognize and respond to the new realities of the American economy in the mid-1970s.

Our assessment of the mainstream of economics is that, like the military, it prepares itself to fight yesterday's battles. Economists have developed intricate models and theories for managing demand according to Keynes' instructions of the 1930s. Economic conditions have changed: we are in the 1970s, soon to be in the 1980s. Supply basically took care of itself over the twenty-five-year rocket ride when the economy was supported by the triad of forces of long-run economic growth. The need of the present is to focus on the supply side of the economy.

Previous chapters of this book have shown how the three basic forces that undergirded the economy have been seriously eroded. Strengths have been transformed into weaknesses. A lessening of societal interest in economic growth has interacted with the energy crisis and the waning storehouse of innovations to weaken the basic thrust of the economy. The trajectory of the rocket is turning down.

During the period of prosperity, the discipline of economics has developed intellectual capital, which is both sophisticated and extensive. Yet, for all of its sophistication this capital doesn't work very well. There can be some question regarding its efficacy during the 1950s and 1960s when the conditions for long-run economic growth were propitious. There is considerably less doubt concerning its inability to confront satisfactorily the new economic realities. Modern economics was never designed for, and is incapable of, meeting the long-run challenges of a slow-growth economy.

During our quarter century of economic growth the economist struck a bargain with the politician. The economist promised the politician a well managed economy and a happy electorate through the use of the economist's fiscal and monetary tools. In return, the politician gave the economists highly prized status, including entry into the highest councils of government. The terms of trade were not very favorable to the economist. He accepted uncritically the short-time horizon of the politician and allowed the politician to unduly influence the intellectual development and orientation of the profession.

As long as the economist could safely assume the basic strengths of the economy, he was correct in emphasizing the short-run trade off between inflation and unemployment. When unemployment was 4 percent and inflation a mere 2 percent, this was a rational world. Recently we have experienced inflation and unemployment rates of near double-digit proportions. Debates that seemed sensible when the sum of the two rates was 6 percent appear ludicrous when the sum of the two rates is as high as 20 percent. Something isn't working, and part of that something is the models, insights, and policy prescriptions of economics. Rather than regarding economic adversity as a spur for critical re-examination of economic dogma, too many economists have called for larger and larger doses of the traditional medicines—more fiscal or monetary policy or the combination of the two—and little else.

Economists have a tremendous investment in obsolete intellectual hardware, which is equally matched by emotional attachment. They are loath to jettison hard-learned and intellectually elaborate theories and models. Economics today must cope with a problem similar to that which it experienced in the 1930s, when the economists baldly ignored the realities of the time and instead held steadfastly to time-honored models and beliefs. As a consequence, economics was soon recognized as being irrelevant and was swept away by the Keynesian revolution—a similar prospect threatens today.

Economics needs to return to the basics: helping society maximize over time what it can receive from a given resource endowment. In part this requires confronting the problems pointed out in the prior set of recommendations. Economists should lead in the effort to mitigate unreasonable expectations. Consumption will have to be more explicitly and inextricably linked to production. All groups in society must be impressed with the direct relation between reward and contribution. No group can continue to increase its economic position without causing inflation, except by increasing its productivity. Kennedy and his economists were right in stressing this fundamental relationship.

The competitive market mechanism must be rejuvenated and more heavily utilized in all sectors of the economy. Competition must be revitalized in the industrial sector and introduced into the growing service sector of the economy. The reason is simple. The competitive market does an exceptional job of securing efficient use of limited resources, especially when compared to nonmarket processes. The role of economists in aiding this spread of competition is most vital.

Many new societal laws have been passed that commit the United States to massive expenditure programs. Before plunging ahead with programs to meet the more stringent standards of the future, the cost of achieving the various objectives must be weighed against the societal benefits to be gained. Inputs from the economics profession are essential for evaluating the extent and nature of our commitment to cleaning up the environment, improving conditions in the workplace, and changing marketplace relationships.

Finally, and perhaps most importantly, economists need to develop models, insights, and policies for managing a slow-growth economy—an economy with increasingly limited and costly resources. In doing so economists must shift their emphasis from manipulating the economy with short-run, demand-oriented policies to studying problems of long-run economic growth which originate on the supply side of the economy. The benefits of the economists altering their attention will be a return to relevance and the opportunity to serve the larger interests of society.

Index

187